# GLOUCESTER

# Fishermen's Wives

## COOK BOOK

### Stories and Recipes

Susan Pollack

First published in the United States
of America by:

Twin Lights Publishers, Inc.
8 Hale Street
Rockport, Massachusetts 01966
Telephone: (978) 546-7398
http://www.twinlightspub.com

ISBN 13: 978-1-885435-61-4
ISBN 10: 1-885435-61-4

10 9 8 7 6 5 4 3 2 1

Photos by Alan Murtagh:
pages 2–3, 4–5, 6–7

Book design by
SYP Design & Production, Inc.
http://www.sypdesign.com

Printed in China

To the wives and families of
commercial fishermen everywhere:
You are the rock upon which all
seafaring communities stand.

# Contents

# INTRODUCTION

*I* first met the Gloucester Fishermen's Wives more than 25 years ago when I was starting out as a reporter. It was 1978, and New England fishermen, still suffering the effects of overfishing by foreign factory ships, were facing the specter of off-shore oil drilling on Georges Bank, the region's prime fishing grounds. I was awed by the fact that the same group of women who had gone to Washington to fight for the US's 200-mile limit law had now joined with conservationists to win an equally momentous battle against offshore oil.

Since its founding in 1969, the Gloucester Fishermen's Wives Association has been a powerful force for the conservation of New England's precious fishing grounds and heritage. The Wives have helped improve safety standards on US vessels; create the first subsidized health plan for fishermen; establish a marine sanctuary at Stellwagen Bank; and protect the health of the oceans and the future of the fisheries that feed us all.

The Wives, many raised by immigrant parents who spoke no English, have cultivated the most influential people in government. Today, if Angela Sanfilippo, the group's intrepid and eloquent long-time president, considers that a proposed regulation will hurt fishermen, she picks up the telephone and calls Senator Ted Kennedy.

Over the years I've interviewed Angela and Lena Novello, an association founder and legendary cook, among others. I've huddled with the Wives at public meetings and savored *scungilli* salad and freshly-caught sea urchin with their families at St. Peter's Fiesta. I've sat in their kitchens drinking espresso, nibbling *biscotti*, and listening to the marine radio crackle out news of offshore storms while the women awaited the safe return of their loved ones—men engaged in America's most dangerous profession—commercial fishing.

The Gloucester Fishermen's Wives Association erected the new memorial that overlooks Gloucester Harbor honoring the "faith, diligence, and fortitude" of the Fishermen's Wives, qualities that arise in part from their strong Sicilian-American, Portuguese, Irish, and Newfoundland cultural traditions.

Food is the centerpiece of any Wives' gathering and, as the women know, it is food that sustains, not only the lives of activists, but those of their families and the stalwart fishing crews who labor at sea. I've never experienced anything like the hush that comes over a table when the pasta course is served.

When I first knew Angela, the Wives regularly met in her kitchen, while her youngest, then a toddler, played nearby. The Wives are consummate cooks as well as dedicated activists. They're passionate about promoting herring and other such under appreciated fish at cooking demonstrations and through their enormously popular spiral bound seafood cookbook. And just mention *bilharacos*, the irresistible Portuguese finger food, or *i dolci*, particularly those from Sicily! *Mamma Mia!*

This book celebrates the Wives' cuisine and politics. I invite you to read the Wives' stories of cooking, courage, and love; to savor the photographs; and to feast on the foods that have nurtured Gloucester's seafaring families for generations.

Buon Appetito!

Susan Pollack
Gloucester, Massachusetts

*Members of the Gloucester Fishermen's Wives Association, from left to right: Nina Groppo, Fina Sanfilippo, Gerri Lovasco, Margherita Pelliccia, Angela Sanfilippo, Mary Jo Montagnino, Connie Condon, Raffaela Terzo, Grace Favazza and Jeanne Gallo.*

Photo courtesy of Sharon's Studio of Gloucester

A quarter century ago, a fisherman's young wife addressed the US Senate on a matter of great urgency to her husband and all New England fishermen: saving the celebrated Georges Bank fishing grounds from offshore oil exploration. To the woman's left and right sat oil magnates eager to exploit the very grounds she sought to protect. Angela Sanfilippo rose, all five feet of her, in her high heels; she adjusted the microphone and began: "We have nothing against the oil companies. Your responsibility is to provide oil. Ours is to feed the nation."

When she finished, Senator Paul Tsongas of Massachusetts, who had convened the hearing, said he would not want Angela as an adversary; even the oil men congratulated her. It was 1980; just three years earlier the Gloucester Fishermen's Wives Association had elected Angela its president, and under her leadership the Wives were transforming a once fledging group into a powerful force for conservation of New England's precious fishing grounds and heritage.

A problem solver with an orator's gift, Angela testified that day, as always, with only the barest notes, jotting down ideas as she listened to the statements of her opponents. She also remembered the words of her paternal grandmother and namesake, a woman so revered in Porticello, Sicily, that people called her Donna Angela. The older woman wrote letters, read, and interpreted legal documents for Porticello's 4,000 residents, many of whom were unlettered. Angela was devoted to this nonna, a village amanuensis, and often accompanied her on her rounds. One day, after interceding on behalf of a local fisherman who had lost his license, Donna Angela whispered to then five-year-old Angela: "Sometimes we must kiss the hands of those who need to have them chopped off."

Hard words, but ones that Angela Orlando Sanfilippo has taken to heart during a long and effective career fighting to protect the fishing way of life so crucial to New England and particularly her adopted Gloucester. Angela is deeply committed to this city by the sea, its fishing community, and fisheries, which have sustained hers and so many other immigrant families for generations.

Angela arrived in Gloucester in 1965, knowing very few words of English, but determined to learn the language—and quickly. She and her parents and siblings had left their native Porticello 18 months earlier, spending the intervening months in Milwaukee, where no one was happy, least of all Angela, who was ignored in school because she could not speak English. Her parents had wanted to return to Porticello, but her father's godson, Tom Brancaleone, also a Sicilian native, encouraged them to resettle, instead, in Gloucester.

To 15-year-old Angela, Gloucester appeared, as if "a fairy tale." The beaches and wharves reminded her of Porticello. And the fish! "We really thought that we were in heaven." says Angela, remembering her first sight of the Brancaleone's kitchen with its "beautiful modern appliances and stainless steel sinks, sinks full of fresh fish. We had not seen fresh fish for 18 months!"

Mariano Orlando, Angela's father, immediately returned fishing and she and her brother, Joe, spent the summer gathering mussels and periwinkles in the rocks below the fishermen's statue. They also dug clams in the flats at low tide. At the time a set of stairs ran from the foot of the statue down to water's edge, providing easy access to this shellfish paradise. Come fall, brother Joe and sister Josephine, both younger than Angela, entered school in grades suitable to their ages. Angela, who was less fluent in English, cried when she heard that school authorities wanted to place the young woman in the eighth grade at Central Grammar School. She insisted on being given a chance at the high school and, after producing prior academic records revealing good grades, she struck a deal. She must learn English by December or be sent to Central Grammar. Angela more than fulfilled her promise, graduating from Gloucester High School in 1969, a member of the National Honor Society and the president of the high school's honors business club.

She secretly applied to the Navy and was accepted, but her parents said, "no." Mariano and Antonina Orlando had encouraged Angela and Josephine to finish high school, but, they would not allow their daughters to go away to college. "As new immigrants, they were not ready for that lifestyle." (Later, Josephine would have to turn down a full scholarship to art school.) And Angela's parents needed her at home, especially now with a toddler to care for—her brother, Vincent, born in 1966. Her mother, Antonina, a skilled seamstress and a private person, did not work outside the home after Vincent's birth.

As the first born daughter of immigrant parents, Angela has always negotiated for her family in the community. She helped her parents to purchase a house and car, schedule doctors' and other appointments, while also translating for them and other non-English speaking relatives, even after she had married and started a family of her own.

In 1970 Angela married her sweetheart, John Sanfilippo, a fisherman and native of Porticello. She was at home with their oldest children, Mary Ann and Dominic, (the youngest, Giovanna, had yet to be born) when she received a telephone call from Lena Novello of the Gloucester Fishermen's Wives Association. Lena needed someone to translate for fishermen during a meeting with federal fishery officials. It was August, 1977, several months after the US's 200-mile

*Angela Sanfilippo testifies at Gloucester City Hall in 1979, the day before going to Washington D.C. to battle oil drilling on George's Bank.*
Photo by Nubar Alexanian

limit had been enacted, and New England fishermen, men like Angela's husband, John, were facing yet another shutdown of the codfish fishery. This was Angela's first meeting and she quickly fingered the problem: In setting codfish quotas fishery managers had ignored social and economic considerations. When she finished speaking, several hundred people applauded. She became an industry advisor to the Northeast Groundfish Multi-species plan, and in December, 1977, the Wives voted her their president.

On Angela's watch, among other accomplishments, the GFWA has helped bring about improved safety standards on US vessels, the end of ocean dumping, a ban on destructive factory trawlers, the first subsidized health plan for fishermen, and a marine sanctuary at Stellwagen Bank. They have erected a statue on the Boulevard honoring fishermen's wives, while also seeking to maintain Gloucester's working waterfront. The Association has also taken an active role fighting for fair but equitable

*Angela's husband, John, on his boat, the* Giovanna.
Photo courtesy of Ed MacKinnon Photography

fishing regulations that rebuild New England's depleted groundfish stocks without putting fishermen out of business. And Angela has taken on another hat as the project manager of the federally-funded Gloucester Fishermen and Families Assistance Center, helping fishermen and their families to find work out-side fishing, even as the GFWA fights to save Gloucester's fishing industry.

During the early years of Angela's tenure as GFWA president, members often met in her kitchen while her youngest, Giovanna, played in the next room. Angela's table became a gathering place for lively conversation and debate, especially during St. Anthony's novena. Angela began offering the novena in 1976, continuing the tradition of both her Sicilian grandmothers. When Angela was a girl in Porticello, she remembers, the streets filled with altars during the 13-day celebration. "My grandmothers, everyone put them outside. The houses were very small and in June it was very hot. They would take down the altars every night and build them back up again in the morning." On the feast day, Donna Angela fed 13 orphans and a priest.

In Gloucester, Angela and John invite family and friends to celebrate the feast day, which follows a novena in which the women meet nightly to sing and pray to St. Anthony. For St. Anthony's feast, John grills fresh mackerel, and sometimes striped bass, caught by his son, Dominic; the Sanfilippos also serve marinated squid or octopus, and a cornucopia of homemade Sicilian sweets. That night Angela and her daughters and her mother prepare a raw pasta sauce all their own—with the freshest tomatoes, basil, garlic and olive oil. They pour this over hot spaghetti, capping a rich and meaningful 13-day celebration.

Angela appeared on "Ciao America," the Public Broadcasting System show, in late 2000. While demonstrating how to prepare a soup with salt cod, Angela spoke with PBS host Mary Ann Esposito about the GFWA's efforts to keep the fishing culture alive.

Politics is in Angela's blood. She may have been groomed for this life at the side of Donna Angela and her father, Donna Angela's son, who was a fisherman's representative in Porticello. Angela is disciplined, organized, and speaks with a passion rooted in her love of place, the fisheries, and fishing families. It seems fitting that this fisherman's wife should celebrate Anthony, the once timid saint who found his voice.

## BEEF NAPOLITANO
SERVES 4

1 lb. fresh mushrooms, sliced
1 28-oz. can ground tomatoes
1/4 cup garlic, chopped
1 tablespoon oregano
1/4 cup fresh basil, chopped
salt and pepper to taste
1 1/3 cups water, divided
2 lbs. beef tips
1/2 cup olive oil
1 teaspoon salt

Place mushrooms in a microwave safe dish with 1/3 cup water. Cook on high for 5 minutes. Rinse, drain and set aside.

In a large bowl, combine tomatoes, garlic, oregano, basil, salt and pepper, and remaining water. Mix well and set aside.

Heat oil in a skillet and sauté beef tips. Remove and place them in the bowl with tomatoes.

Add mushrooms to the skillet and sauté for a few minutes. Add mixture from the bowl to the skillet. Mix well. Cover and cook at medium heat for about 20 minutes, or until beef is tender.

Serve with Italian bread.

Can also be served over cooked white rice.

---

*Note: Many recipes included in this book call for canned crushed tomatoes. I prefer to use Pastene Kitchen Ready Ground Peeled Tomatoes.*

## CALAMARI TRIZZANO
SERVES 5–6

1/3 cup olive oil
2 cups onions, sliced
3 lbs. fresh cleaned calamari, cut into rings
3 tablespoons pine nuts
3 tablespoons raisins
1/4 cup fresh parsley, chopped
2 teaspoons salt
black pepper to taste
1 28-oz. can ground tomatoes
1 lb. spaghetti (optional)

Heat oil in a skillet and sauté onions. Add calamari and sauté until they are golden.

Add nuts, raisins, parsley, salt, pepper, and crushed tomatoes. Cook at medium heat for about 20 minutes. Remove from heat and let sit for 15 minutes.

Serve in individual bowls with Italian bread.

When serving with spaghetti, cook spaghetti according to package directions. Drain and mix with calamari sauce. Sprinkle with Romano cheese.

Can also be served over white rice.

## FESTA SALAD

SERVES 2

1 2-oz. can anchovies in oil (optional)
2 large tomatoes, cubed
10 black olives (Greek or Calamata)
small bunch basil leaves, torn into pieces
1/4 cup onions, chopped
1/2 teaspoon oregano
salt and pepper
1 6-oz. can tuna fish in oil, drained
1/2 cup olive oil
1 tablespoon white vinegar

In a bowl, combine first 6 ingredients. Salt and pepper to taste. Mix well.

Add tuna, oil, and vinegar. Mix well.

Serve over a bed of lettuce and Italian bread. Salmon can be substituted for the tuna.

## GOOD AND SIMPLE MARINARA SAUCE

SERVES 4

1/4 cup olive oil
1/4 cup garlic, minced
1 28-oz. can ground tomatoes
1/2 can water
1/4 cup parsley
salt and pepper

Heat oil in a skillet and sauté garlic. Add crushed tomatoes and water. Stir well. Add salt, pepper, and parsley. Mix well and cook at medium heat for about 45 minutes, stirring often to prevent sticking.

This sauce can be used for any fish dish. For pasta, eggplant, beef, chicken, and pork, add 1/4 cup of minced onion with the garlic and replace parsley with fresh basil.

*The* Giovanna *in Gloucester Harbor.*

*With tuna or salmon, the Festa Salad, made with flavorful olives and anchovies, is a meal all its own.*

## MALANISA SAUCE
SERVES 5

1 head cauliflower, cut into florets
1/2 cup olive oil
2 cups onions, sliced
6 anchovies in oil
1 6-oz. can tomato paste
1/3 cup raisins
1/3 cup pine nuts
salt and pepper
1 cup plain Italian bread crumbs
2 tablespoons olive oil
1 lb. *Bucatini* pasta or linguine

Rinse cauliflower in cold water and then boil in salted water for about 8 minutes.

Remove cauliflower and drain, reserving water for cooking pasta in.

In a skillet, heat oil and sauté onions. Add anchovies and sauté for a few more minutes.

Add tomato paste and sauté, stirring constantly over medium heat. When paste becomes dark red, add cauliflower and mix well.

Add nuts, raisins, and pepper. Allow cauliflower to sauté with all the other ingredients for about 3 minutes.

Add 3 cups of the reserved water. Stir, cover, and cook over medium heat for about 7 minutes.

Place bread crumbs in a skillet with 2 tablespoons of oil. Stir constantly over medium heat. Remove from heat when crumbs are golden.

Cook *Bucatini* pasta according to package instructions using reserved cauliflower water. Drain and return to pan. Mix some of the Malanisa sauce and bread crumbs with the pasta. Serve in individual dishes. Add more sauce to each serving and sprinkle with remaining bread crumbs.

## MEDITERRANEAN SWORDFISH STEAK
SERVES 3

1 lb. swordfish steak about 1/2" thick, cut into 3 portions
1 cup Mediterranean bread crumbs (see page 93)
1/3 cup olive oil
2 tablespoons olive oil
juice from 1 lemon
1/2 teaspoon oregano

Wash fish in cold water and pat dry.

Pour 1/3 cup olive oil into a small bowl and the bread crumbs into another small bowl.

Dip swordfish first in oil and then in bread crumbs, pressing the crumbs into the fish.

Grill swordfish until the bread crumbs are golden, or bake at 400 degrees until golden brown.

In a separate bowl, combine 2 tablespoons oil, lemon juice and oregano. Spoon over cooked fish and serve.

*Mediterranean swordfish steak*

## MARINATED TUNA STEAK

SERVES 3

3 fresh tuna steaks (about 8 oz. each)
1/3 cup olive oil
1/3 cup garlic, chopped
1 tablespoon oregano
juice from 1 lemon
salt and pepper to taste

Rinse tuna steaks in cold water. Pat dry with a paper towel and set aside.

In a deep bowl, add oil, lemon juice, garlic, oregano, and salt and pepper. Mix well. Allow tuna steaks to marinate in the mixture for about 15 minutes on each side.

Place one piece of tuna steak on aluminum foil. Add some of the marinade. Wrap and place on a grill or in a 400 degree oven.

Cook for approximately 15 minutes or until done. Do not overcook.

Serve with salad or vegetables.

## MEDITERRANEAN SHRIMP SALAD

SERVES 6–8

2 lbs. medium shrimp, peeled
1/3 cup olive oil
1 tablespoon garlic, minced
1/4 cup fresh Italian parsley, chopped
juice from 1 lemon
salt and pepper

Wash and dry shrimp. Sprinkle with oil and cook on a grill or in the oven.

In a bowl, mix oil, garlic, parsley, lemon juice, and salt and pepper.

Add grilled shrimp and mix. Let it set for about 10 minutes.

Serve over lettuce leaves with Italian bread.

## MEDITERRANEAN BAKED OR GRILLED LOBSTER

SERVES 4

5 1-lb. lobsters
2 cups Italian seasoned bread crumbs
1/2 cup olive oil

Marinade:
    2 garlic cloves, chopped
    1/4 cup olive oil
    juice from 1 lemon
    1/2 teaspoon oregano

Remove lobster meat from shell using lobster scissors. Wash well and pat dry with a paper towel.

Dip lobster meat in oil and coat with bread crumbs.

Place lobster on the grill at medium heat. Turn a few times. When bread crumbs are golden, remove and place on a platter.

In a small bowl, combine oil, garlic, oregano, and lemon juice. Spoon over lobster and serve.

If baking, place lobster in a 400 degree oven until bread crumbs are golden. Place on a platter and spread marinade over lobsters, and serve.

*Mediterranean baked lobster prepared with a delicate lemon, oil, and oregano sauce.*

## MUSSELS IN MARINARA SAUCE

SERVES 3

5 lbs. mussels
1/4 cup olive oil
1/4 cup garlic, chopped
1 28-oz. can crushed tomatoes
1/4 can water
1/3 cup Italian parsley, chopped
salt and pepper

Heat oil in a skillet and sauté garlic. Add tomatoes, water, parsley, and salt and pepper. Stir and cook for 15 minutes.

Transfer sauce to a large pan and add mussels. Mix well. Cover and cook at medium-high heat until mussels have opened.

Serve in a bowl with toasted Italian bread.

Mussels can be served over spaghetti with grated Romano cheese.

*Statues of St. Peter and Lady of Fatima are carried through the streets of Gloucester during St. Peter's Fiesta.*

## PASTA TRICOLORE

SERVES 5

2 lbs. ripe tomatoes, cubed
8 large garlic cloves, peeled
1/2 cup fresh basil, coarsely torn
2 tablespoons pine nuts (optional)
1/4 cup olive oil
1/3 cup grated Romano cheese
1 teaspoon salt
pepper to taste
1 lb. spaghetti

Drain cubed tomatoes in a colander.

Place garlic, basil, and nuts in a food processor for a few seconds.

Add the tomatoes and chop for a few seconds. Transfer mixture to a large bowl.

Add oil, cheese, and salt and pepper. Mix, cover, and set aside.

Cook spaghetti according to package directions. Drain well and add to sauce in bowl. Mix. If there is not enough juice, add additional olive oil.

Serve on individual plates and sprinkle with Romano cheese.

*Pasta Tricolore*

## SAINT ANTHONY'S BREAD
SERVES 6

1 loaf Italian or French bread
olive oil
grated Romano or Parmesan cheese
2 cups fresh ricotta cheese
pepper

Warm bread in the oven. Slice lengthwise, open-faced.

Sprinkle both sides with olive oil and grated cheese. Press the two halves together. Open again.

Spread the ricotta cheese evenly on one side of the bread.

Sprinkle with pepper and grated cheese again.

Bring the two pieces of bread together.

Cut into 2" pieces and serve.

## PASTA WITH POTATOES
SERVES 5

1/2 cup olive oil
3 cups onion, sliced
3 lbs. Idaho potatoes, cubed
1/4 cup fresh parsley, chopped
salt and pepper
3 cups hot water
1 lb. spaghetti
Romano cheese, grated

Heat oil in a saucepan and sauté onions. Add potatoes, parsley, and salt and pepper to taste. Sauté for about 5 minutes, stirring to prevent burning.

Add hot water and simmer until potatoes are soft. Add more water if necessary.

*During the feast of St. Anthony, elaborate altars are created in the living rooms of many Italian-American Homes. Pictured here is Angela's altar.*

In the meantime, cook spaghetti according to package directions. Drain and mix with potatoes.

Serve in individual bowls. Sprinkle with Romano cheese.

The potatoes can also be served as a side dish with roast pork, chicken, beef, or lamb.

## POTATO FRITTATA
SERVES 3

2 cups potatoes, cubed small
1/4 cup oil with 10% olive oil
3 eggs
1/4 cup grated Romano cheese
salt and pepper
1 tablespoon parsley or basil, chopped

Beat eggs in a small bowl. Add cheese, salt and pepper to taste, and parsley. Mix well. Heat oil in a skillet and cook potatoes until golden. Remove excess oil.

Place skillet back on heat and add egg mixture. Cover and fry on medium heat until done.

When the eggs have formed, turn the frittata over by sliding it onto a plate and putting the skillet on top of the plate, turning the frittata back into the skillet. Let the frittata fry on its other side over low heat. When both sides are cooked, put it in a platter, cut like a pizza, and serve.

Please use caution when turning frittata over to avoid being burned.

## STIR FRY GARLIC CAULIFLOWER
SERVES 5

1 head cauliflower
1/2 cup water
salt and pepper
1/4 cup garlic, minced
1/3 cup oil with 10% olive oil

Remove green leaves from cauliflower. Wash and place in a glass bowl with water and a little salt. Cover and place in microwave for 20 minutes on high. Remove from microwave and let stand for 5 minutes.

Cut cauliflower into chunks.

Heat oil in a skillet and sauté garlic. Add cauliflower and salt and pepper to taste. Sauté until cauliflower is golden.

Remove and place on a platter. Sprinkle with Romano cheese.

Serve as a side dish with fish, steak, chicken, or pork.

## ZUCCHINI SOUP
SERVES 5

5 cups zucchini, peeled and cubed
2 cups onions, sliced
1/4 cup tomatoes, chopped
1/4 cup olive oil
1 teaspoon salt
pepper to taste
1/4 cup cubed Romano cheese

Place zucchini, onions, tomatoes, oil, salt, and pepper in a pot. Cover ingredients with water and bring to a boil. Lower heat and simmer until zucchini is tender.

Add Romano cheese. Mix well and let sit for 10 minutes.

Cubed potatoes and/or cooked Italian sausage may be added.

## TUNA A LA PORTICELLO

SERVES 5

2 lbs. fresh tuna, the central part
1/4 cup Romano cheese, cut into small pieces
1/4 cup fresh basil, chopped
1/4 cup fresh mint leaves, chopped
10 garlic cloves, peeled and cut in half, for stuffing
1/2 cup olive oil
1/2 cup onion, chopped
1/3 cup garlic, chopped
1 6-oz. can tomato paste
1 28-oz. can crushed tomatoes
1 1/2 28-oz. cans water
salt and pepper to taste
1 lb. of your favorite pasta

Rinse fresh tuna in cold water and pat dry with a paper towel.

With a knife, poke a few holes into the tuna and stuff each hole with a small piece of cheese, garlic, and mint. Set aside.

Heat oil in a skillet and sauté the tuna. A wonderful aroma will fill your kitchen! Move tuna to a platter and cover with aluminum foil. Set aside.

Place skillet back on heat and sauté onions and chopped garlic. Add tomato paste and stir until the paste is dark red. Add crushed tomatoes and water, stirring occasionally to blend.

Add salt, pepper, basil, and mint. Cover and let sauce come to a boil. Turn heat down and cook on medium-low for about one hour, occasionally stirring to avoid burning.

Place tuna in sauce and let cook for approximately 30 minutes. Turn off heat and let the tuna sit for another 15 minutes. Remove and place on a platter. Cut into serving size pieces.

In the meantime, cook pasta according to package directions. Drain and mix with sauce. Sprinkle with Romano cheese. Serve tuna and pasta together.

## SPINACH-MUSHROOM SOUP

SERVES 4

2 packages fresh spinach
1 lb. fresh mushrooms, sliced
1/4 cup water
1/4 cup olive oil
8 garlic cloves, chopped
1/2 cup crushed tomatoes
1 teaspoon salt
pepper to taste

Wash spinach well and set aside.

Place mushrooms and water in a microwave safe bowl. Cover and microwave for five minutes on high.

Rinse and drain well. Set aside.

Heat oil in a skillet and sauté garlic. Add crushed tomatoes and cook for 3 minutes, stirring occasionally.

Add mushrooms and cook for another 5 minutes, stirring occasionally.

Add spinach and salt and pepper. Cook for 5 minutes or just until spinach is wilted.

Serve in individual bowls with toasted Italian bread. Sprinkle with Romano cheese.

*Spinach-mushroom soup*

erolama Parco Lovasco grew up during the Depression in the Fort, a Gloucester neighborhood that has long housed the city's newest arrivals. The daughter of Sicilian immigrants, she lived in an apartment building on Commercial Court adjacent to Pavilion Beach. "Most families had six, seven, or eight children," she remembers. "The ocean was our playground. At night we could hear the ocean splashing on our windows. We were that close. I shared a bedroom with two sisters, Ida and Carmella. Sister Mary slept on a sofa and brothers Joe and Tony shared another bedroom. We had running water, but we had to share a bathroom in the hall with another family. We had electricity, but we had no TV, washer, or dryer."

"I had one toy—a rag doll, which my father brought back from California, when he was fishing there. We did get paper dolls sometimes or cutouts if we got a magazine." In one game, Gerri and her sisters played crew to her brother Tony's captain. "Tony would take a piece of a discarded net from my father's boat. We would put clothespins in the middle of the net and (and pretend that they were fish) and draw the fish in."

"We did not have much," says Gerri, "but I can remember the women laughing, men talking, and bread baking. My father used to make soft breads at 4 A.M. and we would wake up to the smell of them. On the cold days, he would make *zabaglione* (eggnog) and *muffoletti* (hot soft breads) for breakfast. He beat the eggs real frothy and then he would put in a little Marsala. He would give each of us some and then we would walk from the Fort to St. Ann's Church or Central Grammar. He would say, 'That will keep you warm.' For Christmas Eve, he made a delicious *bac-cala* (baked salt cod) with celery, onions, potatoes, green olives, and tomatoes."

"My father read a lot and he loved Italian operas. He would read to us and tell us stories, all in Italian. We grew up speaking Italian; we learned English by playing with other children."

"An organ grinder and his monkey came to the Fort to entertain us children. And there was Mr. Fellman with his donut truck. He'd open it up and in one drawer would be jelly donuts and in another, buns. My mother bought one of each. And Minnie, the egg lady, came in her van. She had a farm and she'd bring fresh eggs and live chickens. My father would snap the neck, an oh, it made lovely chicken soup. The best in the world!"

"My mom would not have supper until my dad returned home from fishing. Whether he showed up at 5 or at 9, we would wait; half of us were asleep, but we waited. We had to eat what my mother put on the table. We all had chores to do. Some of us would pick up the plates. My sister was only 6 years old, but my father made her a bench, and she would stand on it and do the dishes, and I would dry them. When we got older, I would give my sister Ida a nickel if she would dry."

"There was a crucifix above my mother's bed. Pictures of Mary and Joseph hung on the walls, and every day she read her missal and said the rosary. We had to go to mass, even if it was below zero. Once a month we could go to the movies. It cost ten cents. You could not go if you did not go to mass."

At age 15, to help support her family, Gerri left school and took a job as a seamstress. "I was called a 'collar girl' as I worked on the collar of the jackets and that was quite a job because of the esquisite detail it required." Then during World War II, she made parachutes for the Mighty Mac Corporation. Her employers, Harold and Dick Bell, were sensitive to the needs of Gloucester's immigrants, sometimes putting up bond for them.

An Irishman sought to date Gerri, but her parents would not stand for it. "We were to marry our own people, the Sicilian, Italian," she says. In 1942, Peter Lovasco, a romantic Italian, successfully wooed her. "My brother Tony pinned a heart on my pillow. It had my name on it with a tiny ruby. Peter had given him the heart made out of a seashell." He gave Gerri her first kiss (she was 18) and soon after, at a dance, he proposed. Her parents were "tickled pink." They knew that he was from a good family and that his father was the captain of his own boat, a big plus. World War II delayed the wedding. Peter volunteered, and the Army, recognizing his expertise in fishing and navigation, assigned him to the Amphibians for special training. In 1943 Peter was sent home because of foot problems. They wed the following year.

"On my wedding day my mother told me to go downstairs and talk to my sister," Gerry remembers. "I didn't know anything about sex, but I learned very quickly. And we had the best honeymoon." The couple visited, among other places, New Jersey, where, says Gerri, "my cousin Minnie gave us her bedroom. When we were in bed, we heard music getting closer and closer. There were guitars and mandolins. Before we knew it, our bedroom door opened and all our relatives walked in and serenaded us. We laughed and said, 'get out of this room!' We got dressed and left the room. You can't believe the banquet that my cousin had prepared! We ate and we drank and I blushed and blushed. My husband blushed more than I did."

The year that they married, Peter became captain of the 78-foot eastern rig trawler *St. Joseph*, a family boat built for his father, Captain Jerome Lovasco, and named for the patron saint. Peter had only an eighth-grade education, but was known as a skilled

*Gerri Lovasco along with Grace Favazza and others at a supermarket cooking demonstration.*

and tenacious fisherman. He fished for scup, shrimp, lobster, and groundfish, steaming as far east as Nova Scotia, and down the east coast of Florida. "He was not afraid to venture to new grounds. He would go out in bad weather, but he knew where to go," says Gerri. When others were returning to port, he would often be going out to fish." Some called him Crazy Pete, but often he was the one who would get the high prices.

He also endured at least one close call. In 1961, returning from a long fishing trip and deprived of sleep, he turned over the wheel of the *St. Joseph* to his mate, who ran the boat onto the rocks at Milk Island. Peter managed to get out a May Day over the marine radio. The US Coast Guard rescued him and his four crewmen, and while the men managed to salvage $11,000 worth of electronics, they lost the boat. Despite this he fished another quarter century aboard a new boat that he built and christened, the *St. Joseph II*. Today, while suffering from Parkinson's, his bone fishing needles, which built and mended many nets, still fly as he makes hammocks. "If I do say so the hammocks are quite good," says Gerri. Her brother, Tony, became the owner of a fish processing company, Ocean Crest. Two other brothers became fishermen. Gerri's and Peter's children, Jerry, Milena, and Gayle, pursued other careers, encouraged in part by their mother's insistence that they get the education that she could not.

A co-founder of the Gloucester Fishermen's Wives Association, Gerri has played an important role in the organization since its earliest days. She was among the Wives who traveled to Washington with a dory in tow to testify on behalf of the US's 200-mile limit law; she lent a crucial hand in the Wives' highly successful cookbook, *A Taste of Gloucester: A Fisherman's Wife Cooks*, and she remains active in the Association today.

## JUST SIMPLY GREAT PICKLED HERRING

SERVES 6–8

5 tablespoons butter
2 onions, thinly sliced
2 cups bread crumbs
1/4 cup grated Parmesan cheese
4 tablespoons parsley, chopped
3 potatoes, thinly sliced
2 lbs. pickled herring, cut into serving portions

Heat skillet with butter and sauté onions until transparent. Set aside.

In a bowl, mix together bread crumbs, cheese, and parsley. Set aside.

In a well greased baking pan, layer onions, potatoes, herring, and bread crumbs. Salt and pepper to taste. Repeat until all ingredients are used. Bake at 350 degrees for 40 minutes or until done.

## OCEAN CREST
### Stuffed Fillet of Sole Rollé

SERVES 8–10

3 lbs. fillet of sole or flounder
2 cups crushed Ritz crackers
1/2 cup seasoned Italian bread crumbs
2 tablespoons onions, chopped
1/4 cup grated cheese
1/2 cup celery, chopped
1/4 cup tomato juice
1 stick butter or margarine (melted)
1 10 3/4-oz. can cream of mushroom soup
1 cup water

In a bowl, combine crackers, bread crumbs, onions, cheese, celery, tomato juice, and margarine.

Divide fish into equal portions. Place a heaping tablespoon of bread crumb mixture onto each fillet. Roll each fillet and place in a greased baking dish. Set aside.

Mix together cream of mushroom soup and water. Pour mixture over fillets.

Bake at 375 degrees for 15 minutes or until fillets are flaky. Serve hot.

*The Gloucester Fishermen's Wives Association in 1979. Front row, left to right: Angela Sanfilippo, Lena Novello, Margaret Favazza, and Josie DiLiberti. Back row, left to right: Gerri Lovasco, Grace Favazza, Phyllis Orlando, Rosalia Loiacono, Mary D'Amico, Vincie Parisi, and Peg Sibley.*
Photo by Michael Lafferty

## DOG STAR
### Crispy Coconut Wolf fish
SERVES 6

1 cup all purpose flour
1/2 cup corn flour
1/2 cup toasted coconut
1 lb. wolf fish cut into bite size pieces
1 egg
1 tablespoon milk
oil for frying

Mix together first 3 ingredients.

In a separate bowl, combine the egg and milk. Beat well.

Dip fish pieces in egg mixture and then in flour mixture, covering all sides of fish.

Heat oil in a skillet and fry fish until golden brown.

Drain on paper towel or brown paper bag.

Serve with duck sauce.

## BEER BATTER FISH G. LOVASCO STYLE
SERVES 6–8

2 lbs. fish fillet (any white fish)
4 tablespoons Bisquick
1/2 teapoon salt
1 egg
1/2 cup beer (do not use light beer)
oil for frying

Lightly coat fish with Bisquick.

In a bowl, beat together salt, eggs, and beer until smooth.

Dip fish into batter and fry until golden brown— about 2 minutes on each side.

## GERRI'S ZUCCHINI BAKE
SERVES 4–6

5 eggs
1 cup Bisquick
3/4 cup grated Romano cheese
1 large carrot (sliced thin, use grater)
1 small onion, diced
1/4 cup vegetable oil
4 cups zucchini, pealed and sliced thin
1/4 cup fresh parsley, chopped

In a large bowl, beat eggs. Add Bisquick, cheese, carrots, onions, and oil. Mix well. Add zucchini and parsley. Mix until blended.

Pour mixture into a greased 13" x 8" baking pan. Bake at 350 degrees for 45 minutes or until done.

Serve hot or cold.

## GREEN SAUCE

2 anchovies, cut into pieces
2 tablespoons capers, chopped
1 cup parsley, chopped
2 garlic cloves, minced
1/4 cup olive oil
1/4 cup wine vinegar
dash of pepper

Combine all ingredients. This sauce is great over fish, meat or pasta.

*The statue of St. Peter is carried through the streets of Gloucester during St. Peter's Fiesta, the four-day summer celebration honoring this patron saint of fishermen.*

Photo courtesy of Giacomo Terzo

## ITALIAN TUNA DIP

2 garlic cloves, minced
1 1/2 cups sour cream
1 envelope Italian salad dressing mix
2 teaspoons lemon juice
1 cup mayonnaise
1 6-oz. can white tuna, drained and flaked
2 hardboiled egg whites, chopped
2 tablespoons fresh parsley, chopped
1 small carrot, grated

In a bowl, combine garlic, sour cream, dressing mix, and lemon juice.

Gradually add mayonnaise. Mix well.

Add tuna, eggs, parsley, and carrot. Mix well.

Set in refrigerator for 12 hours.

Serve with crackers or raw mixed vegetables.


## GAYE'S STRAWBERRY TRIFLE
SERVES 10–12

1 pint fresh strawberries or 1 package frozen (not in sugar)
1 13-oz. jar strawberry preserves
1-lb. pound cake, cut into 1" cubes
1/2 cup fruit liquor (optional)
2 small packages instant vanilla pudding (prepared using package directions)
1 16-oz. container Cool Whip
1 cup slivered almonds, for garnish
4 strawberries for decoration

In a bowl, mix together preserves and fruit. Let sit for 30 minutes.

Sprinkle liquor over pound cake.

In a glass trifle bowl, layer cake, preserves, pudding, and Cool Whip. Repeat layers until all ingredients are used. Top with sliced strawberries and almonds.


## DOG DAY HOT SOUP
SERVES 10–12

3  13 3/4-oz. cans of beef or chicken broth
6 cups water
3 onions, diced
2 bay leaves
2 cups celery, chopped
2 tablespoons celery leaves, chopped
2 cups potatoes, diced
1 cup carrots, diced
2 fresh tomatoes, chopped
1/4 cup fresh parsley, chopped
2 1/2 lbs. wolf fish or any firm white fish, cut into chunk size pieces
salt and pepper to taste

In a large pot, combine broth, water, onions, and bay leaves. Bring to a boil.

Add celery, potatoes, carrots, and tomatoes. Cook until tender.

Add fish and parsley. Salt and pepper to taste.

Cook for 15 more minutes, or until fish flakes easily.

Serve with garlic bread.

## EELS SICILIAN STYLE
### (a day before Christmas or New Years)
SERVES 4

4 tablespoons olive oil
1 cup onions, chopped
3 or 4 garlic cloves
1/2 lb. mushrooms
1 cup water—more if needed to cover eels
2 lbs. eels, skinned and cut into 2 1/2" pieces
4 tablespoons fresh parsley, chopped
2 fresh basil leaves
1 cup red wine
salt and pepper to taste

Heat oil in a skillet and sauté onions.

Add garlic, mushrooms, wine, and water. Simmer for 10 minutes.

Add eels and simmer for 10–15 minutes.

Add parsley, basil, and salt and pepper to taste.

Serve with fresh Italian bread.

## CAPTAIN PETER'S FAVORITE MOLASSES COOKIES
MAKES APPROXIMATELY 40 COOKIES

6 cups all purpose flour (King Arthur's)
1 teaspoon allspice
1 teaspoon ground cloves
1 teaspoon baking powder
1 teaspoon pepper
3/4 cup sugar
1/2 cup butter or margarine
3 eggs
1 12-oz. bottle molasses
zest from 2 oranges
1 cup walnuts, chopped
sesame seeds

In a bowl, combine flour, allspice, cloves, baking powder, and pepper. Set aside.

In a separate bowl, mix together sugar, eggs, butter, molasses, zest, and walnuts. Add flour mixture and blend by hand until you form a soft dough.

Lightly grease hands and surface with oil. Divide dough into 4 or 5 balls. Roll each ball into logs, about 1 1/2" thick. Roll in sesame seeds.

Cut diagonally into 1 1/2" pieces. Transfer onto a cookie sheet lined with parchment paper.

Bake at 350 degrees for 10–15 minutes.

"I'm the cookie lady," says Josephine Taormina as she sweeps a tray of plump, bronze confections out of the oven and places them on a cooling rack. These are Josephine's famous cookies, moist, light, and now maddeningly, mouthwateringly, fragrant. Their sweetness floods her sunny kitchen on this chilly morning.

Here in her spacious Gloucester cucina, with its Blodgett oven and industrial grade mixer, Josephine, a 44-year-old mother and fisherman's wife and daughter, carries on the culinary art of *i dolci* passed down by her Sicilian forbears. She slides another tray into the oven, then sits down at a long Formica table. Reaching into a large stainless steel mixing bowl, she breaks off a piece of dough and rolls it into a narrow log. She divides that into smaller pieces, then twists each one into a perfect loop, which she places on a greased baking sheet.

"What I enjoy about these cookies is that they remind people of their past," says Josephine, who is as bright and gracious as she is down-to-earth. "People say to me, 'Oh, my God, my grandmother used to bake these.' Or 'When my mother was alive, she made them. I miss it.' The cookies bring back memories, of the holidays, when their families got together."

Trupiano's Superette, among others, sells assortments of Josephine's cookies tied in the red, white, and green of the Italian flag. She also fills special orders and, because she does not advertise, people know her cookies only by word of mouth.

Sweets such as Josephine's are central to Sicilian cuisine and culture. Not only did Sicily inherit the sweet tooth of the Saracens and easy access to sugar cane, observes food historian Waverly Root, author of the classic, *The Food of Italy*. In Sicily, "sweets embody most clearly the ritual role of food, forgotten elsewhere, which through the ages has bound it to magic, superstition, and religion."

Indeed, in Sicily, *i dolci* are tied to feast days and other holidays. In Josephine's parents' hometown of Trapetto, near Palermo, traditionally women got together in early December to make their celebrated *cucciddata*, Christmas fig cookies. Josephine's mother and grandmother baked large batches of the delicate confections in wood-fired brick ovens. They made their own *marmellata di fico*, fig preserves, the essence of the cookie, from fruits grown on their own trees. They flavored their fig cookies with freshly-grated cinnamon, lemon, and orange, a practice that Josephine follows today.

Josephine's cookies embody the flavors of Sicily—not only the figs grown in every yard, but the lemons, honey, and especially the almonds, said to have arrived with the ancient Greeks. Almonds are the basis of many Sicilian sweets, including Josephine's *amaretti*, a macaroon-like confection for which she grinds her own almond paste, and her almond *biscotti*.

Josephine began baking cookies at age ten, guided by her mother, Mary Costanzo, and her Aunt Fina. "My first job was to take the cookies out of the oven when they were done. I graduated to applying the frosting and jimmies. I enjoyed it and it came naturally." (Nowadays before Christmas Josephine's mother, her Aunts Fina and Lia, her mother-in-law, Grace, and her friends Giuseppa and Pina all come to Josephine's house for a day to help make *cucciddata*. "All of the women are fishermen's wives and members of the GFWA," Josephine is a longtime board member.)

It is now mid-morning, and the first batch of vanilla cookies have cooled enough for Josephine to apply frosting. She spreads the creamy glaze, consisting of confectioner's sugar and milk, one cookie at a time. "There are no shortcuts." The vanilla frosted cookies are, hands down, "the star of the show; they're always the most popular," says Josephine. The vanilla cookie provides the basis for a half-dozen other confections, including Josephine's fanciful pink and green "watermelon slice," her cinnamon and nut twist, applesauce cookie, and orange marmalade slice. The basic recipe, a stripped down version of *cucciddata*, is Mary Costanzo's. "People used to rave about my mother's vanilla cookies. I told her, 'we should sell them!'"

Josephine was born and grew up in Gloucester, the oldest of four children. "My mother was pregnant when she arrived so you can say I'm an Italian import." Her childhood home was on Beach Court near Pavilion Beach, where she spent summers "watching the boats go in and out. I was always interested in the fishing industry because of my family."

Josephine's father, Salvatore (Toto) Costanzo, owned and operated the fishing vessel *Vincie and Josephine* until retiring ten years ago. Josephine's husband, Tony, fished with him for many years. Today Tony works as the engineer on the Boston-based dragger *Almah-Rosa*. He arrived in Gloucester, from Sicily, at age 14. Tony and Josephine have three children, Dominic, 22, Grace, 18, both of whom are in college, and Sal, 14, who is a freshman at Gloucester High School and on its football team.

"I've never worked fulltime because Tony was always away fishing. My main interest was to be there for my children. I knew I couldn't replace Tony, but I tried to be mother and father to my kids," says Josephine.

"When we were first married Tony would be gone up to 12 days; he'd come home for a day or two and spend most of that time down at the boat mending nets and doing other repairs. Sal, our youngest, has had the best of his father because the time that fisher-

*Rosandra Brancaleone and Josephine's son, Salvatore, depict the Gloucester Fishermen's Wives statue at the Horribles Parade.*

men spend at sea has gotten shorter and shorter. In fact, with increasing restrictions, fishing is no longer a fulltime job. Tony saves his fishing days till winter, when prices are best. He takes other jobs—painting, carpentry, landscaping—to fill in." Now with less family income from fishing, Josephine is considering expanding her cookie making into a fulltime business.

Her family has always been close. Six Januarys ago, her father suffered a serious accident while putting away Christmas ornaments. His injuries were so severe that doctors had little hope that he would survive. Josephine, her mother, her sister, Fay, two brothers, Anthony and Jack, and their spouses virtually lived at Massachusetts General Hospital for 40 days until Salvatore Costanzo emerged from intensive care. During the long recovery and rehabilitation that followed the family never left his side and they and everyone they knew prayed for him. Today at age 75, he is healthy and fit. His recovery is considered a miracle, in no small part a testament to the devotion of a loving family. "We always say he survived," says Josephine, " because we were there day and night."

## RICE WITH PEAS AND MUSHROOMS
SERVES 4

1 cup rice
2 teaspoons salt
2 bouillon cubes (optional)
1/4 cup olive oil
1 onion, chopped
1 lb. frozen peas, thawed and rinsed
4 oz. fresh mushrooms, sliced
pepper

Bring 4 cups of water to a boil in a saucepan. Add rice and 2 teaspoons salt. Add 1 teaspoon salt if using cubes. Follow rice-cooking instructions, but remove from heat 2 minutes before it is done. Stir rice often and add more salt to taste if needed.

Rinse with cold water and drain using a colander. Put aside.

Heat oil in a skillet and sauté onion.

Add peas, mushrooms, and salt and pepper to taste. Sauté six minutes or until mushrooms and peas are cooked. Remove from heat.

Combine mushroom and pea mixture with rice. Add more olive oil if necessary. Salt and pepper to taste if needed.

## TOMATO SAUCE WITH HAMBURGER

1 lb. ground beef
2 teaspoons olive oil
1/2 onion, chopped
2 28-oz. cans ground tomatoes
1 teaspoon salt
pepper
basil leaves

In a skillet, sauté beef until browned. Drain.

Heat oil in a saucepan and sauté onion.

Meanwhile, purée tomatoes in a blender and add to onions. Fill tomato cans 1/2 full with water and add to sauce.

Salt and pepper to taste. Add hamburger. Cook on medium heat for 45 minutes, stirring occasionally. Add basil leaves 5 minutes before sauce is done.

This is a great sauce for ravioli, tortellini, rice, and pasta.

## MEXICAN DIP

8 oz. cream cheese, softened
1/2 cup onion, chopped
1/2 cup tomato, chopped
1/2 cup green pepper, chopped
1/2 cup black olives, sliced
8 oz. Mexican cheese blend
1 cup salsa

Spread cream cheese evenly on the bottom of a baking dish. Layer tomato, onion, green pepper, and salsa. Top with Mexican cheese blend and sliced olives.

Cover with foil. Bake at 325 degrees until cheese melts. Great dip for tortilla chips or crackers!

## BAKED CHICKEN PARMESAN

SERVES 4–6

2 tablespoons olive oil
1/2 onion, chopped
1 14-oz. can ground tomatoes
1/2 can water
salt and pepper to taste
4 chicken breasts
Italian seasoned bread crumbs
olive oil for dipping
shredded mozzarella

Heat oil in a skillet and sauté onions.

Add tomatoes and salt and pepper. Simmer for 15 minutes.

In the meantime, dip chicken in olive oil and seasoned bread crumbs. Place on a baking sheet. Spread sauce over chicken.

Bake at 350 degrees for approximately 1/2 hour or until chicken is done.

Remove from oven and top with mozzarella. Place chicken back in the oven until mozzarella melts.

*Fishing vessels harbored at Jodrey's State Fish Pier.*
Photo by Peter Prybot

## ALMOND BISCOTTI

MAKES 2 DOZEN

1 1/2 cups sugar
1 teaspoon baking powder
2 teaspoons orange extract
2 teaspoons lemon extract
3 eggs
2 cups flour
8 oz. whole almonds (lightly toasted)
1 teaspoon vegetable oil
1 egg, beaten (for brushing)

In a bowl, combine sugar and baking powder. Add orange and lemon flavoring. Mix.

In a separate bowl, beat 3 eggs and add to mixture.

Mix well.

Add toasted almonds and then flour. Mix together.

Divide dough into two portions. Lightly coat hands and surface with vegetable oil. Roll dough out into 1 1/2" thick logs. Transfer logs onto a cookie sheet lined with parchment paper.

Brush each log with beaten egg.

Place logs on a greased cookie sheet, about 3 inches apart.

Bake at 350 degrees for 20–25 minutes or until golden and firm to the touch. Cool on rack.

Cut logs diagonally into 1" thick slices and put the pieces back in oven for 10 minutes to toast.

## AMARETTI

MAKES 2 DOZEN

1/2 lb. almond flour
1 cup flour
1 cup sugar
2 teaspoons shortening
1/2 teaspoon baking powder
2 egg whites
2 teaspoons almond extract
candied cherries, cut in half

In a bowl, mix together almond flour, flour, sugar, and baking powder. Add shortening and work well. Add almond extract.

Beat egg whites to stiff peaks and add to mixture.

Lightly coat hands with vegetable oil and roll dough into a log. Cut into 1" rounded pieces. Roll each ball in sugar to coat. Place on greased baking sheet. Top cookies with cherries.

Bake at 300 degrees for 7 to 8 minutes or until lightly golden. Move from cookie sheet to cooling rack.

## PISTACHIO CAKE

1 box yellow cake mix
4 eggs
1/2 cup vegetable oil
1 box instant pistachio pudding
1 cup water
1 1/4 teaspoons almond extract
green food coloring, (optional)
1/2 cup peeled pistachios, slightly crushed

Filling
1 28-oz. container of Cool Whip
1 box instant pistachio pudding
1 teaspoon almond extract
crushed pistachios

In a bowl, combine above ingredients. Use an electric mixer to mix on low speed until moistened. Beat at medium speed for 2 minutes.

Grease and flour sides and bottom of a bunt pan.

Pour batter in pan and bake at 350 degrees for 35 to 40 minutes. Cool in pan or wire rack for 15 minutes.

To prepare filling, beat together Cool Whip, pudding, and almond extract.

Cut cake in half and fill with pistachio filling. Put other half on top. Reserve some of the filling to use as frosting.

Frost the entire cake with remaining filling. Top with crushed pistachios.

Photo courtesy of Jeff Rotman Photography

Grace Misuraca Favazza is a woman of faith and action. She is also a survivor. As fisherman's wife, daughter, and sister, she knows the perils of commercial fishing, America's most dangerous occupation. She also knows the ordeal of waiting for a loved one to return from the sea. Twenty-six years ago, her oldest brother, Vito Misuraca, and five other fishermen left Gloucester aboard the 86-foot dragger *Captain Cosmo* and never returned.

Misuraca was 62 and had wanted to retire. "But destiny called," says Grace. "The *Captain Cosmo* was short one man, and so the skipper came to my brother's house. He promised to get him home and that this would be his last trip. My brother was so good-hearted he said, 'yes.'" And that was the last time we saw him. There was a gust of wind and the radio wasn't working that good. The boat was full and it tipped over."

The crew of the wooden fishing vessel included the 21-year-old cousin of Grace's husband, Peter. The young fisherman planned to return in time for his sister's wedding. Grace remembers: "I was in the hallway waiting for the bride to walk down the aisle. She was in tears because her brother wasn't there. They had left his clothes on the top of the bed. I told her, 'this is your wedding day. Everything will be okay. When the weather is bad they sometimes pull into a port.'"

But the next day, says Grace, "we heard that the *Captain Cosmo* was lost at sea. I couldn't understand why my mother was screaming. Then I realized that Vito was on the boat." For a month, Grace's mother waited and prayed, hoping for some word. But "the captain and crew were lost, without a trace. It was terrible. It touched the whole city of Gloucester. A few

weeks later, the *Alligator* went down" with all three men aboard.

A wiry 76-year-old with dark curly hair, Grace is both resilient and energetic, two traits that have helped her to weather the fishing life. She grew up in the Fort surrounded by other children of Sicilian parentage. Her family was large but close knit; she has four sisters and six brothers. Her parents, Gantano and Giovanina Misuraca, came from Terrasini. Her father was a fisherman. Grace's mother "never left the house. Like many women of her generation, she stayed at home except for religious events—baptisms, first communions, weddings, wakes. When their husbands came back from fishing, the wives might get dressed up and go out with them."

Grace's mother "was always cooking, washing, and cleaning. She baked everything—the bread, the pizza, all from scratch. We never ate anything frozen or canned. We couldn't afford much meat, but we always had fresh seafood from the boat, we had vegetables and fruits, and we had chickens that she raised herself."

Grace was born the year that St. Peter's Fiesta began, in the Fort, as a neighborhood celebration. Sicilian-Americans including her future father-in-law, Peter Favazza Sr., Leo Linquata of the Gloucester House Restaurant, and Benjamin Curcuru, a fish plant owner and then "the richest man in Gloucester" helped Captain Salvatore Favazza to realize a dream of bringing the fishermen's saint to Gloucester. Captain Favazza commissioned a Charlestown artist to sculpt the turquoise-robed statue of St. Peter, which today looks out onto Rogers Street and the harbor from the St. Peter's Club. Originally it

*De-icing is important to the stability of fishing vessels and imperative to the safety of the crew.*
Photo by Nubar Alexanian

stood in the window of Peter Favazza & Sons, a marine supply store in the Fort. To allow residents a better view of the statue, a half-dozen strong fishermen carried the 700-pound icon through the narrow waterfront streets. During the early years of Fiesta, an altar "as high as a cathedral" stood beside Grace's mother's house, at 19 Commercial Street. "Priests, altar boys, and, even Cardinal Cushing" stopped in this house, where Grace grew up and spent the first 12 years of her marriage.

As a boy Peter Favazza Jr. had worked as a bookkeeper at his father's store, which furnished the boats with canned goods and other food as well as oil, gear, twine, and marine hardware. He began fishing after he and Grace married, on Easter Sunday, 1960. Peter worked as a cook on offshore vessels that were at sea

for 10 to 12 days at a time. He was away for the births of two of their children. Having grown up in a fishing family, Grace took this in stride. "I was used to that life," she says.

Peter and Grace enjoyed a long and happy marriage. He died in 1995. Six months later Grace made a pilgrimage that they had hoped to make together, to Terrasini, Sicily. "I was able to make the trip because Angela [Sanfilippo] could not; she had booked a trip with the Sicilian Society. She called me up and off I went to Sicily. I took my mother's birth certificate and marriage license, and went to the city hall in Terrasini. I found out where she and my father were born, lived, baptized, and married. I saw where my father went fishing and where my mother went swimming. And I saw the mountains. Whenever my mother got upset

*Sorting fish after hauling back the net.*
Photo courtesy of Jeff Rotman Photography

with us 11 children she would say, in Italian, that she was going to take off and go stay in the mountains."

"I don't want to sit around watching TV," says Grace. "I want to be helpful." Back on Cape Ann, she became certified as a nurse's aid, enabling her to administer to the elderly and homebound. She volunteers at the Home Care facility at Blackburn Office Park, as an election pole watcher while also taking an active role in, among other civic and religious organizations, the Mother of Grace Club, the Madonna della Rosario Society, the St. Peter's novena committee, and the Gloucester Fishermen's Wives Association, of which she is a founder and longtime member. One of her fondest memories is of going to Washington, D.C. for the Smithsonian Institution's salute to the GFWA.

Grace and Peter raised four children: Sabrina, Thomas, Gina, and Peter, a designer who created the Gloucester Fishermen's Wives Association logo that appears on aprons, t-shirts, and potholders.

## SALMON PIE

SERVES 6

2 lbs. potatoes
3 tablespoons olive oil
1 medium onion, chopped
1 stick butter
1 12-oz. can pink salmon
2 piecrusts
milk for brushing

In a large pot, boil potatoes until done. Drain and set aside.

Heat oil in a skillet and sauté onions. Set aside.

Place the potatoes in a bowl and mash. Add onions, butter, and salmon. Mix together gently.

Grease the bottom of a glass pie plate. Place crust in pie plate and add salmon filling.

Cover with pie crust. Pinch edges. Brush top of crust lightly with milk.

Bake at 350 degrees for 35–40 minutes or until piecrust is golden brown.

Cool and serve.

## SEAFOOD CHOWDER

SERVES 8–10

1/4 lb. salt pork fat, cut into small pieces
1 medium onion, chopped
2 lbs. potatoes, peeled and cubed
1 10-oz. can clams
1 lb. haddock, cut into chunks
1 lb. scallops
1 lb. shrimp, peeled
1 stick butter
1 can evaporated milk
1 pint light cream
salt and pepper to taste

In a large pan, sauté pork at low heat until it is crispy. Add onion and sauté.

Add potatoes and clams with juice. Add enough water to cover ingredients. Then add haddock, scallops, and shrimp.

Bring to a boil and then turn heat down and simmer for 15–20 minutes or until done.

Add butter, evaporated milk, and light cream. Salt and pepper to taste. Simmer until you are ready to serve.

## BOURBON BALLS

MAKES APPROXIMATELY 3 DOZEN

5 dozen vanilla wafers, crushed
2 tablespoons cocoa
1 cup confectioners' sugar
1 cup walnuts, finely chopped
3 tablespoons bourbon or brandy
3 tablespoons corn syrup

In a large bowl, combine wafers, cocoa, sugar, and walnuts.

Add bourbon and corn syrup. Mix well.

Form into 1" balls and then roll in confectioners' sugar.

Store in covered container 1 to 2 days to age.

## AUNT SUDA'S RICOTTA BALLS

MAKES 2 DOZEN

2 1/2 cups self-raising flour
1 16-oz. container ricotta cheese
6 eggs
4 teaspoons sugar
1 teaspoon vanilla
oil for frying
cinnamon and sugar mix

In a bowl, combine first 5 ingredients.

In a pot, heat enough oil for frying ricotta balls. Drop dough by tablespoons into hot oil, starting slowly. Allow balls to roll in the oil. Remove when golden brown and drain on paper plates. Continue until all dough is used.

Roll in cinnamon and sugar mix.

## AUNT JENNY'S ITALIAN CHRISTMAS FRUIT CAKE

2 cups flour
3/4 teaspoon baking powder
1/4 teaspoon baking soda
1/4 teaspoon cream of tartar
1 1/2 cups walnuts, chopped
1 1/2 cups sugar
3 small eggs
1/2 cup corn oil
1/4 cup milk
1 small jar candied red cherries
1 small jar maraschino cherries

In a bowl, combine flour, baking powder, baking soda, cream of tartar, and walnuts.

In a separate bowl, beat sugar, eggs, oil, and milk. Combine with flour mixture. Add cherries.

Grease and flour a bundt pan. Pour batter into pan and bake at 350 degrees for 45 minutes.

After the cake has cooled, remove from pan and sprinkle with confectioners' sugar.

## DECEMBER 13TH ST. LUCY PUDDING

1 lb. wheat berries

Cream Pudding:
4 cups milk, divided
6 teaspoons cornstarch
1 cup sugar, divided
1 teaspoon vanilla
1/2 cinnamon stick
rind from 1/2 lemon

Garnish:
Grated chocolate bar with almonds and cinnamon.

Soak wheat berries in water for 2 hours. Rinse and place wheat in a large saucepan. Fill the pan 3/4 full with water. Cook on medium-high heat, stirring often, for 1 hour or until tender. Drain and set aside.

In a bowl, combine 1 cup milk and the cornstarch. Stir until dissolved. Set aside.

In a saucepan, warm the remaining 3 cups of milk. Add the sugar and stir until it is dissolved. Add the cinnamon and lemon rind.

Slowly add cornstarch mixture to the saucepan. Stir continuously until milk begins to thicken. Bring to a boil and cook for about 3 minutes. Remove from heat.

Turn half the pudding onto a large platter. Spread wheat berries over the pudding. Pour remaining pudding over the wheat. Garnish with grated chocolate bar and cinnamon.

## PUMPKIN BREAD

3 1/2 cups flour, sifted
1/2 teaspoon baking powder
2 teaspoons baking soda
1 1/2 teaspoon salt
1/2 teaspoon nutmeg
2/3 cup walnuts
2/3 cup dates, chopped
2 3/4 cups sugar
2/3 cup margarine
4 eggs
1 cup canned pumpkin, beaten
2/3 cup water

In a bowl, combine flour, baking powder, baking soda, salt, nutmeg, walnuts, and dates.

In a separate bowl, combine sugar, margarine, eggs, pumpkin, and water. Combine with flour mixture.

Grease and flour two loaf pans. Bake at 350 degrees for 1 hour and 20 minutes. Remove from oven and cool on rack before removing from pans.

## RICOTTA CAKE

1 yellow cake mix
1 32-oz. container ricotta cheese
1/2 cup sugar
3 eggs
1 teaspoon vanilla

Follow the package directions for the cake mix. Pour batter into a 9" x 13" pan.

In a bowl, combine cheese, sugar, eggs, and vanilla. Pour mixture over batter.

Bake at 375 degrees for 60 minutes. Cool and then dust with confectioners' sugar.

## SWEET CREAM FILLING

1/3 cup sugar
2 teaspoons cornstarch
1/2 teaspoon salt
2 cups milk
2 egg yolks, slightly beaten
2 teaspoons margarine or butter, softened
2 teaspoons vanilla

In a saucepan, combine sugar, cornstarch, and salt. Gradually stir in milk. Cook over medium heat, stirring constantly until mixtures thickens and begins to boil. Continue stirring for one minute.

Gradually add egg yolk and continue boiling for one minute. Remove from heat and stir in margarine and vanilla. Cool.

This filling may be used in place of frosting for any cake or pastry.

## BREAKFAST STRATTA
SERVES 4–6

6 slices bread, cubed
1 lb. cooked and skinned sausage, chopped
6–8 eggs, beaten
1 teaspoon mustard
2 cups milk
1 cup yellow cheddar cheese
1 cup mozzarella

Place bread in a buttered 9" x 13" baking dish. Add sausage.

Combine eggs, mustard, and milk. Pour over bread. Top with cheese.

Bake at 350 degrees for 1 hour.

Refrigerate overnight or 2 hours.

Great for breakfast guests!

## CHOCOLATE BALL COOKIES
MAKES 4 DOZEN

1 chocolate fudge cake mix
2 cups flour
1 teaspoon cinnamon
1 teaspoon ground cloves
4 eggs
1/2 cup oil
1–2 cups walnuts, crushed

In a bowl, combine cake mix, flour, cinnamon, and cloves. Add eggs and oil. Mix well.

Roll mixture into 1" balls and place on a greased cookie sheet.

Bake at 350 degrees for 8–12 minutes. Balls will still be soft.

Cool and frost with white or chocolate frosting. Sprinkle crushed nuts over the cookies.

## SESAME COOKIES
MAKES 4 DOZEN

5 cups flour
1 1/2 cups sugar
5 heaping tablespoons shortening
5 teaspoons baking powder
3 eggs (beat in blender)
1 tablespoon vanilla
sesame seeds

In a bowl, combine flour, sugar, shortening, and baking powder. Beat eggs and vanilla in a blender. Add to dry ingredients. Work dough by hand until it is soft in texture. Form balls using 1 teaspoon of dough. Roll in the sesame seeds.

Bake at 375 degrees for 10 minutes. Turn cookies over and bake an additional 10 minutes.

*Felicia Wharf*
Photo by Peter Prybot

## SQUASH CAKE

3 cups flour
1 teaspoon baking powder
1 teaspoon baking soda
1/2 teaspoon salt
2 teaspoons cinnamon
1 12-oz. bag chocolate chips
1 cup walnuts, chopped
4 eggs
1 1/4 cups oil
2 cups sugar
1 can squash
2 teaspoons vanilla

In a bowl, combine flour, baking powder, baking soda, salt, cinnamon, chocolate chips, and walnuts.

In a separate bowl, cream together eggs, oil, sugar, squash, and vanilla. Combine with flour mixture.

Pour batter into a greased and floured tube pan. Bake at 350 degrees for 1 hour and 10 minutes.

## PIZZELLES

YOU NEED A PIZZELLE MACHINE!

6 eggs
3 1/2 cups flour, sifted
1 1/2 cups sugar
1 cup margarine, melted and cooled
1/2 teaspoon anise
1 teaspoon vanilla
4 teaspoons baking powder

Beat eggs while gradually adding sugar. Beat until smooth.

Add margarine, anise, and vanilla.

In a bowl, combine flour and baking powder. Add to egg mixture. Dough will be sticky enough to drop by spoonfuls and will have a consistency of toothpaste.

## ITALIAN COOKIES

4 cups flour
4 teaspoons baking powder
1 teaspoon cinnamon
1/2 cup toasted almonds
4 eggs, beaten in blender
1 1/2 cups sugar
1 cup shortening
1/2 teaspoon vanilla

In a large bowl, combine flour, baking powder, cinnamon, and almonds.

In a separate bowl, beat together eggs, sugar, shortening, and vanilla. Combine with flour mixture and mix well to form a soft dough.

Roll dough out into an "S" shape or a braid. Bake at 375 degrees for 10 minutes or until golden brown.

## CHRISTMAS CHERRY NUT CAKE

8 oz. cream cheese, softened
1 cup butter, softened
1 1/2 cups sugar
1 1/2 teaspoons vanilla
2 1/4 cups flour, divided
1 1/2 teaspoons baking powder
1 8-oz. jar red maraschino cherries, drained and cut in half (or 4 oz. green and 4 oz. red candied cherries)
1/2 cup walnuts, chopped
2 eggs

In a bowl, cream together cream cheese, butter, sugar, and vanilla until soft. Add 2 cups of flour.

Add eggs, one at a time.

Mix in remaining 1/4 cup of flour. Fold cherries and nuts into batter.

Pour into a well greased 9" x 13" pan and bake at 325 degrees for 1 hour or until done.

## BREAD PUDDING

2 cups warm milk
2 teaspoons butter
2 cups day old bread, cubed
2 eggs, separated
1/3 cup sugar
1/8 teaspoon salt
2 tablespoons brandy
3 tablespoons sugar (for meringue)

In a saucepan, melt butter in milk.

Pour the mixture into a bowl with the bread.

In a separate bowl, beat egg yolks. Add sugar, salt, and brandy. Combine with bread mixture.

Pour mixture into a 9" round cake pan and bake at 350 degrees for 35–40 minutes or until done.

Beat egg whites until stiff. Slowly add 3 tablespoons of sugar to egg whites.

Spread meringue over the baked pudding. Return pudding to the oven and bake for 10–15 minutes or until delicately browned. Serve warm or cold.

## DELICIOUS HOMEMADE PANCAKES
SERVES 2

1 cup flour, sifted
2 teaspoons baking powder
1/4 teaspoon salt
1/4 teaspoon cream of tartar
2 eggs, separated
1 tablespoon sugar
1 cup milk
1 teaspoon almond extract or any flavor you prefer
1 1/2 teaspoons sugar

Sift together flour, baking powder, salt, and cream of tartar 4 or 5 times.

In a separate bowl, beat the egg yolks and sugar. Combine with flour mixture. Slowly add milk and beat until smooth.

Beat egg whites until stiff. Beat in extract and 1 1/2 teaspoons sugar. Delicately fold into flour mixture. Avoid deflating the egg whites.

Pour onto hot, lightly greased griddle and cook until done.

## CITRUS ZUCCHINI BREAD

1 1/2 cups flour
2 teaspoons baking powder
1/2 teaspoon salt
1/2 teaspoon baking soda
1/4 teaspoon nutmeg
1/2 teaspoon cinnamon
2 eggs, beaten
1/2 cup vegetable oil
1 cup sugar
1 cup grated zucchini
1/2 cup orange juice
grated peel from 1 lemon
1/2 cup walnuts, chopped

In a bowl, sift together flour, baking powder, salt, baking soda, nutmeg, and cinnamon.

In a separate bowl, combine eggs, oil, sugar, zucchini, orange juice, and lemon peel. Combine with dry ingredients. Add nuts.

Pour batter into a greased loaf pan and bake at 350 degrees for 55 minutes or until done.

## FRIED RICOTTA BALLS

MAKES 2 DOZEN

2 cups flour
2 teaspoons baking powder
1/3 cup sugar
6 eggs, beaten
1 15-oz. container ricotta cheese

In a bowl, sift together flour and baking powder 3 times.

In a separate bowl, combine sugar and eggs. Combine with flour mixture. Fold in ricotta and mix well.

Heat enough oil in a deep frying pan to fry the dough. Drop dough by teaspoons into hot oil. Fry until golden brown. Drain on paper towels. Roll in a sugar and cinnamon mixture or honey. Serve hot.

## CRUSTLESS CHEESECAKE

1 lb. ricotta cheese
1 lb. cream cheese, softened
1 1/2 cups sugar
4 eggs
1 tablespoon lemon juice
1/4 teaspoon vanilla
3 tablespoons cornstarch
3 tablespoons flour
1/4 cup butter, melted
1 pint sour cream

For topping:
1 package frozen strawberries
2 tablespoons cornstarch

Press ricotta through a sieve. Place in a bowl and blend with cream cheese using an electric mixer.

Add sugar, beating it in gradually. Beat in eggs, one at a time.

Stir in lemon juice, vanilla, cornstarch, flour, and melted butter. Blend until smooth. Blend in sour cream.

Cover the bottom of a cheesecake pan with parchment paper. Pour batter into pan and place in a cold oven. Turn oven on to 325 degrees and bake for one hour. Do not open oven door. Turn oven off and leave cake in oven for an additional 2 hours.

Remove from oven and place on rack. Do not remove from pan until completely cold.

Topping: Strain one half of the frozen strawberries. In a pan, combine strained strawberries with cornstarch. Heat until thickened. Combine mixture with unstrained strawberries. Spread on top of cheesecake.

## BROCCOLI AND CAULIFLOWER PUFFS

SERVES 6–8

1 bunch broccoli
1 head cauliflower
1 cup Italian breadcrumbs (see page 93 for home-made bread crumbs)
4 eggs, beaten
4 cups vegetable oil

Wash cauliflower and cut off stems.

Wash broccoli. Cut off stems and slice crowns in half.

Dip broccoli and cauliflower in egg and breadcrumbs. Fry in hot oil until golden brown.

*Good Harbor Beach*
Photo by Michael Lafferty

## CAPONATA

SERVES 4–6

2 lbs. eggplant, cubed
salt
8 tablespoons olive oil, divided
2 celery stalks, finely chopped
1 medium onion, finely chopped
1 14-oz. can Italian plum tomatoes, chopped
10 large green olives, pitted
2 tablespoons capers, minced
4 anchovy fillets or 3 salted anchovies, rinsed and dried
5 tablespoons red or white wine vinegar
2 tablespoons pine nuts
6 fresh basil leaves

Place eggplant in a colander and sprinkle with salt. Set aside for 1 hour.

In a skillet, heat 4 tablespoons of oil and gently cook the celery for about 15 minutes before adding the onion. Remove celery and onion with a slotted spoon when onion is soft.

Add remaining oil and eggplant. Cook for about 10 minutes, stirring constantly.

Add tomatoes, olives, capers, anchovies, vinegar, sugar, and a little pepper to taste.

Return celery and onions to the skillet. Simmer for about 15 minutes. When the mixture has thickened, add pine nuts and basil and allow to cool.

# ESTRELA da CONCEIÇAŌ GONCALVES BORGES RANDAZZO

strela da Conceiçaō Goncalves Borges Randazzo serves a Christmas meal in Gloucester that combines the culinary traditions of her native Portugal and of Sicily, the home of her husband's family. Her brother, cousin, in-laws—more than 40 family members enjoy the feast, which includes the traditional Portuguese *bacalhau* (baked salt cod), *caldo verde* (kale soup), *arroz doce* (rice pudding), and *bilharacos*, (the irresistible deep fried pumpkin or squash balls), all of which Estrela enjoyed as a girl, plus lasagna and *spiedini*, a rolled meat dish from Sicily.

*Bachalhau* is the main entree, a fitting choice for a fishing family. Estrela is the daughter, granddaughter, and wife of fishermen. When she was growing up, her father salted and dried the cod he caught in their garage here in Gloucester, a practice carried over from their home in Figueira da Foz, in coastal Portugal. Nowadays, Estrela buys the salt cod. Her recipe was passed down from her mother and grandmother. After soaking the cod overnight, she boils it with potatoes, sautés onions and garlic, then layers everything in a baking pan along with black olives. She garnishes the dish with fresh parsley.

Usually Estrela prepares a beef roast with potatoes as another entree. Melissa, 21, her oldest, makes the *spiedini* based on a recipe provided by her paternal grandmother, Giuseppa Randazzo; the lasagna recipe is also Giuseppa's.

The Christmas meal always begins with *caldo verde*. To make the soup, Estrela combines potatoes, onions, and *chorizo*, a tomato base, and a little salt pork for flavor, later adding the kale. Estrela may also serve Little Neck clams steamed in white wine and garlic and olive oil or baked stuffed shrimp as appetizers.

The fruit and cheese courses follow. "The Portuguese are very big on fresh fruit after dinner," and the holiday meal is no exception. Estrela will serve apples, oranges, bananas, whatever fruit looks best, followed by a soft round goat cheese, which she sprinkles with salt and pepper.

Coffee and brandy follow, and then, guests turn their attention to the dessert table. There's Estrela's rice pudding, flavored with lemon peel and made with whole milk (and no eggs), a gigantic meringue called *Molotov* and sometimes flan. On the dessert table you will also find *bilharacos*, an essential in any Portuguese holiday gathering. Guests will nibble on these warm sweet fritters all evening. Estrela makes them with corn flour and sometimes squash. Pumpkin is also a traditional ingredient.

Estrela was born in Figueira da Foz, known for its fishing and sandy beaches. She and her parents, Joao Pereira and Alzira Goncalves Borges, emigrated to Gloucester in 1972, when she was ten. Her grandfather and uncle were already here. Soon after arriving, she was placed in a bilingual class with ten Italian students and one other Portuguese speaker, her cousin. "I learned to speak Italian before English!" laughs Estrela.

Estrela continued to speak Portuguese at home, soon becoming trilingual. She graduated from Gloucester High School in 1980 and attended business school in Boston, completing a two-year program in ten months. She put her business skills to work in the offices of a car dealership and a lawyer and at the Cape Ann Savings Bank. More recently she has served as a translator at sites including Addison Gilbert Hospital. A firm believer in bilingual educa-

*Antonino Randazzo's day boat, the* Skimmer.

tion, she has taken part in a Massachusetts education program for children of migrant workers from Brazil, Portugal, and Italy. "It's difficult for a child who does not understand the English language. There's a lot of talk about cutting out bilingual education, but it serves a child in learning the basics."

Estrela met her husband, Antonino, in her bilingual class. He had also arrived in Gloucester, from Sicily, in the early 1970s. The two did not like each other then, but several years later Estrela's cousin showed Antonino her photograph. He called her. "My father was very strict. I wasn't allowed to go out." They fell in love, married, and have three children, including, besides Melissa, Isabella, 12, and Peter John, nine.

Antonino owns and operates the 41-foot *Skimmer*, a day boat. He now works single handed; with increasing regulations and limited allowable days at sea, he cannot afford to take a mate. Estrela accepts the difficulties and uncertainties of the fishing life, but she does not want her son to follow this path.

"Many people think that fishermen earn a lot of money," says Estrela. Apart from the clear dangers of being at sea in all kinds of weather, people "forget how difficult the fishing life is. The men work very hard. The work is stressful. When the fishermen come home they have to unload the fish and worry about the prices. They have to do any work that needs to be done to the boat, repair any damage, replace equipment. It's not easy to be a fisherman's wife and daughter."

To most of the world, there are 1001 ways to cook chicken. Well, to the Portuguese, there are 1001 ways to cook salted cod fish. Here is one of the most popular ones:

**BACALHAU A GOMES DE SA**
**(Salted Cod baked Sa Style)**
SERVES 8–10

1 1/2 lbs. salted cod
6 potatoes
4 onions, sliced
4 garlic cloves, crushed
1/2 cup extra virgin olive oil
salt and pepper to taste
1/2 cup white wine
1 tablespoon fresh parsley, chopped
4 eggs, boiled and cut into circles for garnish
1/2 cup Portuguese black olives
parsley for garnish

Place fish in a pot and cover with water. Allow fish to soak overnight.

Remove fish from water and place in a large pot. Cover with water and bring to a boil.

In the meantime, place potatoes in a pot of boiling water and cook until done. Peel and cut into circles.

While potatoes and fish are cooking, heat oil in a skillet and sauté onions and garlic until golden brown. Salt and pepper to taste.

Add wine and chopped parsley. Simmer for about three minutes. Put aside.

Drain cooked fish and remove any skin and bones.

Place potatoes and fish in layers in a casserole dish. Top with onions and garlic.

Bake at 300 degrees for 10 minutes or until done. Remove from oven and garnish with eggs, olives, and parsley.

**ARROZ DOCE**
**(Sweet rice pudding)**

2 cups water
peel from 1 lemon
4 cups rice (Arborio is the best)
1–1 1/4 cups of sugar
1 gallon whole milk (approximately)
1 teaspoon vanilla
cinnamon for garnish

In a large pot, bring water and lemon peel to a boil. Add rice and stir.

In a separate saucepan, keep milk warm at all times. Here's the trick: while rice is cooking you have to keep adding the warm milk, stirring at all times. As the rice begins to grow, it will absorb the milk. That's why you need to keep adding milk. (It will feel like your arm is about to fall off, but it's worth it!) Continue cooking for 30–45 minutes. Taste rice to be sure it is fully cooked.

Remove from heat. Add sugar and vanilla, stirring evenly. Adjust sugar and vanilla to taste.

Pour into individual dessert dishes, or do it the old-fashioned way by pouring the pudding onto a large platter.

Garnish with cinnamon when pudding is completely cooled.

## BILHARACOS

MAKES 4 DOZEN

4 1/2 lbs. butternut squash, peeled and cut into pieces
peel from 1 lemon
1 1/2 cups brown sugar
3 cups corn flour
3 eggs
1/3 cup aguardente (whisky)
cinnamon and sugar
oil for frying

The night before making the bilharacos, place squash in a pot of salted water and boil until cooked. Drain and set overnight.

The next day, combine squash, lemon peel, brown sugar, flour, eggs, and aguardente in a bowl.

Knead dough very well and shape into small balls.

Heat enough oil in a pot to fry the bilharacos. Drop the bilharacos into the oil and fry until cooked. Drain on a paper towel and roll in a mixture of sugar and cinnamon. Eat them while they're hot!!

## CHRISTMAS EVE TRADITIONAL DINNER
### Bacalhau Cozido com Grelos  (Boiled Cod Fish with Greens)

SERVES 4–6

2–3 lbs. salted codfish or cod fish cheeks
6 potatoes
2 bunches rapini greens
4 eggs
olive oil
fresh garlic, minced
Portuguese black olives

Place fish in a pot and cover with water. Allow fish to soak overnight.

Place potatoes in a pot of boiling water and cook until they are almost fully cooked. Place fish in the pot for the remaining time. At the same time, add a couple of eggs to boil and eat with the fish. Drain. Peel and slice eggs.

Place enough water in a separate pot to boil greens. Salt and pepper to taste. Boil greens until they are cooked. Drain.

Place fish and potatoes on a large platter. Add greens to the platter and garnish with sliced eggs.

The platter is put in the middle of the table and everyone serves themselves. We garnish our own plates with olive oil and minced garlic to bring out the flavor of the fish. Add some olives and you're ready to eat. It's really good!

"My father would make wine for Christmas," Nina Benson remembers. On Christmas Eve, Nina, her parents, and her eight siblings celebrated with a feast following midnight mass. Her parents, Sicilian immigrants from Terrasini, brought to Gloucester their own rich regional cuisine. Her father saved the wine skins and her mother boiled them with sugar and made a kind of molasses.

"When we got home from church—we would walk all the way from the Fort to St. Ann's Church and back—we would have sausages that my mother had made and then cooked in wine. We'd also have fish, whatever my father had caught."

For dessert, Nina's mother rolled out a sweet dough. "She fried it and we dunked it in the molasses. Sometimes we also had *sfinge*, deep-fried fritters (we made them with cream of wheat) or we had chickpea turnovers."

"We didn't have much money," says 80-year-old Nina, but I didn't know it because we were happy. I had wonderful parents. My mother went out of her way to share; there'd be nine of us kids at the table. She'd buy a bag of cookies for a quarter and she'd divide them evenly. When my father would come from fishing, he loved to bake. He would bake big muffins. He'd use only one or two eggs to a whole pan. Eggs were scarce. He would make pancakes right on the stove; we had an old-fashioned coal stove in the basement."

Nina compares her father to a loaf of bread, an essential food in every Italian home. "Bread is soft; bread you can bend. My father was kind and gentle. He never yelled or screamed at us. We never had any of those bad words in our house. But then in his old age—after my mother passed away, he lived with my husband and me and our children for 22 years—he started to swear. He had Parkinson's and was suffering."

When Nina was growing up, she (and everyone she knew) marveled over the story of her father's entry into the United States. During the later years of World War I, Salvatore Favazza and a fellow sailor in the Italian Navy were rescued by the *SS Bostonian* after their ship struck a mine and sank. The two men endured five days in a life raft; three of their companions died. Salvatore spent three months in Brighton Marine Hospital; he did not return to his native Sicily until many years later, after he had become a US citizen.

Nina was born in Gloucester in 1924. She graduated from eighth grade, but dropped out of high school to work at a tunafish processing plant. Her older sister, Grace, worked there, too. "When I was 16, I was working for 48 cents an hour. When I was first married I got $1 hour."

Nina met her future husband, Louis Benson, in 1942 at the Mariner's Fish Company, where the two worked cutting and packing fish. Like Nina, Louis had been born in Gloucester and raised in an immigrant family. His was from Nova Scotia. The two became friends and then fell in love, marrying in 1943, when Nina was 19. Soon after, Louis entered the Service. When he returned from World War II, he began fishing.

"We were living at 5 Fort Square and from our house I got to know the boats going out and coming in just by looking at them. Our house faced the ocean. I would start cooking his dinner. I lived upstairs in my mother's apartment. I would see his

*Louis and son Sam on the* Peggy Bell.

boat coming in. I could even hear him hollering at me from the window. I remember hearing, 'look Louie, I see your wife waving her drawers at you!' I'd been hanging clothes on the line."

"Louie never made big money, but he was a good worker. Lena Novello could tell you that." For many years Louie worked on Lena's husband's, Joe's, boat, the *Vincie N.* "He really loved that boat. They could depend on him for a lot of things. He knew everything. When young fellows would come aboard the boat, they would look up to Louie like a father. Louie would teach them what to do."

But the fishing life is hard, and money was tight. On Louis's crewman's share, it was hard to make ends meet and support a growing family. Bad weather and

poor fish prices aggravated the situation.

"When I got married I would work off and on. I would work a year or so and then take off for six months. But as soon as Louie came home from a fishing trip, he would give me those eyes. He never wanted me to do any special cleaning—we had to take off. If I was working, he would drink. If I wasn't home he would say, 'what am I going to do alone?' So we sat down and made a deal: when he came home we would go out together. We would go to different restaurants or we would go shopping. He snapped out of it. His life just changed. He was wonderful. He loved to drive and had a good sense of direction. He would look at a map and try to find places like Santa's Village in New Hampshire. In the later years, we went

*Ready for the haul.*
Photo courtesy of Jeff Rotman Photography

everywhere—to Florida, New York, and to California twice by car, once for six weeks and another time for seven weeks."

In 1967, Nina's family sold the house she had grown up in at 5 Fort Square. Birdseye had bought the surrounding land in order to expand. "We were the last holdouts, the only house left standing in the middle of emptiness. My father said, 'Nina when it's time to move, you move.'" The family sold and moved to Addison Street, in town, ending a long era in the Fort." Nina had lived by the water there, as a fisherman's daughter, wife, and as a mother, for more than 40 years.

Nina and Louis had two sons, Frank and Salvatore, twin daughters, Elizabeth and Joann, and another daughter, Susan. A sixth child died in a tragic accident when a toddler. The family also suffered personal tragedy when the dragger *Captain Cosmo* sank in 1978. A nephew, Salvatore Grover, age 30, was aboard and lost at sea.

A mother, grandmother, and great grandmother, Nina is also a longtime member of the Gloucester Fishermen's Wives Association. She has contributed recipes to their cookbook, while also accompanying Lena Novello to fairs, supermarkets, and seafood festivals to demonstrate how to cook fish.

## CATFISH SOUP

SERVES 8–10

2 lbs. catfish, cut into 2" pieces
1/2 cup flour
1/2 teaspoon salt
1 cup corn oil for frying
3 tablespoons olive oil
1 onion, sliced
1/2 cup celery, chopped
1 28-oz. can crushed tomatoes with purée
1/2 cup water
1/2 teaspoon sugar
1/3 cup raisins (optional)
1/2 cup green or black olives, sliced (optional)

In a bowl, combine flour and salt. Dredge fish in flour mixture and set aside.

Heat corn oil in a skillet and fry fish until flaky. Drain on paper towels and set aside.

Heat the olive oil in a skillet and sauté onion and celery. Add tomatoes, water, and sugar, raisins, and olives. Simmer for 10 minutes.

Add fish and simmer another 5 minutes. Salt and pepper to taste.

## BAKED SOLE

SERVES 3–4

1 lb. sole or any white fish, cut into individual portions
1 egg
1/2 cup milk
1 cup Italian bread crumbs
chopped parsley, to taste
Parmesan cheese, to taste
salt and pepper to taste

In a small bowl, combine egg and milk. Beat well.

In a separate bowl, combine bread crumbs, chopped parsley, grated Parmesan cheese, and a little salt and pepper.

Dip sole in egg mixture and then in bread crumbs.

Bake at 400 degrees for 20 minutes or until flaky.

## EASY VEGETABLE SOUP

SERVES 4

4 cups cut up zucchini
1 14-oz. can crushed tomatoes
4 potatoes, cubed
1 small can peas
1/4 teaspoon basil
1 onion, chopped
2 teaspoons oil
3 cups water
salt and pepper to taste

Heat oil in a saucepan and sauté onions. Add remaining ingredients and cook for about 25 minutes or until vegetables are soft.

## MANICOTTI CRÊPE STYLE

SERVES 4

1 cup flour
1 egg, beaten
1 cup milk
oil
1 lb. ricotta cheese
1/2 cup mozzarella cheese, grated
basil or parsley, chopped, to taste
1 26-oz. jar of your favorite spaghetti sauce

In a bowl, wisk together flour and egg. Add a little milk at a time until all the milk is used. Mixture will be thin.

Heat a 6" frying pan with a little oil. Once warmed, pour 1/2 cup of mixture into the pan. Spread evenly. Cook slowly. When done, slide off pan onto wax paper. Repeat until all batter is used. Set aside.

In a bowl, combine cheeses and basil.

Place filling mixture down the center of each manicotti and lap over each end.

Spread some of the sauce over the bottom of a baking dish. Arrange manicotti in dish. Pour sauce over the top.

Bake at 350 degrees for 20 minutes.

## BAKED RICE HAMBURGER WITH SAUCE

1 16-oz. container ricotta cheese
1 egg, beaten
1 teaspoon parsley, chopped
2 cups Parmesan or mozzarella cheese, grated
2 tablespoons milk
1 lb. hamburger, browned and drained
1 cup cooked rice
1 26-oz. jar spaghetti sauce, divided
salt and pepper

In a bowl, combine ricotta, egg, parsley, cheese, and milk.

In a separate bowl, combine hamburger, rice, 1/2 jar of sauce, and salt and pepper to taste.

Place half of the hamburger mixture in a baking dish. Layer with half of the cheese mixture, followed by remaining hamburger mixture, and then remaining cheese mixture.

Bake at 350 degrees for 30–35 minutes.

## POLISH KIELBASA DINNER

SERVES 6

3 tablespoons oil
1/2 cup onion, chopped
2 cups water
2 cups crushed tomatoes or tomato sauce
1/2 teaspoon basil
1/2 teaspoon baking soda
salt and pepper to taste
1/4 teaspoon ground cinnamon
1 10-oz. package frozen brussels sprouts or cabbage
1 14-1/2 oz. can carrots
1 14-1/2-oz. can potatoes
1 lb. kielbasa

Heat oil in a large pot and sauté onion.

Add remaining ingredients except the kielbasa. Bring to a boil. Turn heat down and simmer for 20 minutes. Add kielbasa and simmer for another 15 minutes.

## FRIED FISH

SERVES 3

1 egg
1/4 cup milk
1 cup corn flour
1/2 teaspoon garlic powder
1/2 teaspoon parsley
salt and pepper
1 lb. white fish, cut into 2" pieces
1/2 cup oil

In a bowl, combine egg and milk. Beat well.

In a separate bowl, combine corn flour, garlic powder, parsley, and a little salt and pepper.

Dip fish in egg mixture and then flour mixture.

Heat oil in a skillet and fry fish until each side is golden brown.

## FRIED SCALLOPS

SERVES 4

1 lb. scallops
1 egg, beaten
1/2 cup corn flour
1/2 cup flour
salt and pepper

Beat egg into a small bowl.

In a separate bowl, combine corn flour, flour, and a little salt and pepper.

Dip scallops in egg and then flour mixture.

Heat enough oil in a skillet to fry scallops. Fry scallops in oil until golden brown.

## EASY CHEESE CAKE

1 ready-made graham cracker crust
 8 oz. cream cheese, softened
1/3 cup sugar
1 cup sour cream
1 teaspoon vanilla
1 8-oz. container frozen whipped topping
fresh strawberries for garnish

Beat cream cheese until smooth. Gradually beat in sugar. Blend in sour cream and vanilla.

Fold in whipped topping.

Spoon mixture into crust and chill 4 hours. Top with strawberries.

## ANISE COOKIES

MAKES 3 DOZEN

dash of salt
4 eggs
1 1/2 cups sugar
1 teaspoon anise extract
4 cups flour

In a bowl, combine salt, eggs, sugar, and anise. Beat well.

Place flour in a large bowl and make a well. Add egg mixture and combine. Cover in plastic wrap and chill for 30 minutes.

Divide dough into 2 balls and roll each into a 1 1/2" log.

Bake at 350 degrees for 20 minutes or until golden brown. Cut into 1" thick slices.

"I don't have a master's degree. All I've got to offer is four generations of fishing," says Lena Novello, the intrepid 87-year-old matriarch of the Gloucester fishing community. The daughter, sister, wife, and mother of fishermen, Lena has inspired several generations of Gloucester women to work together to protect their invaluable fishing heritage. Nearly 30 years ago she led a small band of fishermen's wives to Washington to fight for passage of the United States' 200-mile-limit law. "The Fishermen's Wives began because the foreigners were coming in here and taking our fish," she says. "They had huge ships and didn't even throw a fish overboard for the seagulls."

A founder of the Gloucester Fishermen's Wives Association and a longtime activist, Lena does not mince words. This bright-eyed grandmother is known for her forthright manner and wry humor. During the Wives hard-fought (and successful) campaign to prevent oil drilling at the celebrated Georges Bank fishing grounds, a Texas oil executive confronted Lena: "He comes up to me after the hearing and says: 'fish and oil go good together.' I says: 'I know they do.' 'So, why didn't you say that?' he asks. 'Olive oil, vegetable oil, cod oil, not crude oil, not oil from the rigs!'"

Lena has served as the Wives' indefatigable culinary resource, institutional memory, and lynchpin. A tireless promoter of New England fish, she has been a driving force behind the Wives' fabulously successful cookbook, *The Taste of Gloucester: A Fisherman's Wife Cooks*; the book, originally published in 1976, in cooperation with the League of Women Voters, has sold more than 200,000 copies and gone through eight printings, serving as an important promotional tool and fundraiser for the Association.

"When we were working on the book," Lena remembers, "they would set up tables in my dining room. I'd be cooking the fish and the women from the League would test it—hake, squid, skate, pollock. Many people think you cook all fish the same, but each fish needs to be cooked in its own way. Skate wings can be fried, baked, or cooked with garlic sauce."

At Lena's urging, the GFWA applied for and received grants to popularize what were once called underutilized species. "Pollock is just as good as expensive haddock. It has more dark meat, but when you cook it, that disappears," says Lena. "We would take a frying pan with us. We went around to supermarkets, fish stores, nursing homes, and seafood shows showing people how to cook the fish." Once named *Yankee* magazine's "cook of the month," Lena has never tired of cooking for the Wives or of championing domestic seafood.

Lena was born and has lived her entire life in this New England port city that is so permeated by the sea. Her parents settled in Gloucester during the height of Italian immigration in the early years of the 20th century. Like many of his countrymen, her father, Salvatore Parisi, stopped first in the Midwest to work on the railroad, went to Boston to fish, and then fell in love with Gloucester.

"One day, my father and his crew couldn't get back to Boston because of the weather so they tied their boat to the wharf in Gloucester Harbor. 'They've got beaches and wharves right at your back door, just like in Sicily,'" he told the family. Not long after the Parisis settled in a waterfront section of Gloucester known as the Fort, so named because it was once the site of a Revolutionary War installation. It has since housed the city's new arrivals. When Lena's parents arrived, The Fort was an Irish enclave, soon to give way to the Italians. It was a place where Lena's father put his handkerchief up on the clothesline at night and got up early in the morning to check to see which way the wind was blowing.

As the oldest daughter in a family with nine children, she had to quit school in seventh grade to help her mother run the household and take care of the younger children. Since she was bilingual (her parents spoke only Sicilian) they relied on her to negotiate for them in the community. She regularly helped her father to purchase equipment and supplies for the boat and once she assisted him to buy a new engine.

Lena grew up in a two-family house, at 69 Commercial Street surrounded by other fishing families and by fish processing. Her house was at the foot of the Fort's tallest hill, where O'Donnell-Usen then processed cod-liver oil. Across the street from her house, under a shed awning, fishermen mended their nets. Living in the Fort then, everything was delivered: "the milk, the bread, the pastries, the meat, the linoleum, the pots and pans were all delivered to your door," Lena remembers. "Everybody raised their own chickens. When my father was seining he would salt the mackerel for the winter months. If he caught cod, he would also salt it."

Lena's father and uncle owned everything together, shared everything, from the Commercial Street house to the fishing vessel, *Fanny Powers*, and a hammer. "They even bought their first electric iron together and a hatchet together!" says Lena. "I used to fight with my cousin as to who would wash which half of the outhouse."

"I used to ask my father, 'why don't we buy our own house?'" Lena's father insisted that a boat was a better investment: "With a boat you can buy a house, but with a house you cannot buy a boat." In 1930 Salvatore Parisi built a new boat. Lena's brothers and cousins were old enough to become full crew mem-

*Lena Novello appearing on the* Good Day! *show.*

bers, and the family did not want to risk in this most dangerous occupation having all its men on one vessel. Salvatore had planned to name the new vessel after his father, Joseph Parisi, but an unforeseen event changed that.

While the dragger was under construction, in nearby Essex, Salvatore, two brothers, and a cousin borrowed a small fishing boat from a neighbor, Mr. Frontiero. Seconds before the men lowered the net into the water, the boat's kerosene engine exploded, igniting a huge blaze. The men managed to grab onto pieces of the wreckage, even though suffering severe burns. Lena's brother, Ben, a strong swimmer, offered to swim for help. But Lena's father asked, "Who are you going to find out here? Which way will you swim?" Salvatore urged the men to stay together. "If we're going to die, then we will all die together." He raised his eyes skyward and beheld a vision of St. Rosalie, the patron saint of Palermo, Sicily. Seconds later, the fishermen spotted the vessel that rescued them. Salvatore christened his new boat, *St. Rosalie*, also giving this name to a daughter who was born soon after.

In 1938, at age 21, Lena married Joe Novello, also a fisherman. To her marriage she brought the skills she had learned negotiating for her father and helping

*Vessels* Vincie N. *and* Rose Marie
Photo by Alan Murtagh

to run the household for her mother. "My husband would call me from the boat to order parts for the engine. I was always there for him. I would tell the icehouse to get the ice ready for him. And I would go with him as I did with my father. If he couldn't get the right price for a part, he would pick out what he wanted and then tell me that he was going to check the car. That was my cue to dicker with the salesman to get a better price."

During the warm summer months, when the men were painting the boat, at Gloucester Marine Railways, "We would carry iced coffee and lemonade and spaghetti and meatballs down to them," so that the men wouldn't lose valuable fishing time. Till recently Lena and Joe's son, Salvatore, (Sam) had fished the family's stalwart *Vincie N.* She had been the last working eastern-rig trawler in the port. Today Sam runs a former shrimper, the *Captain Novello*, continuing to fish for whiting, cod, and haddock, despite ever-increasing restrictions.

The family has donated the 60-year-old *Vincie N.* to the Gloucester Marine Heritage Center. With the active efforts of Sam and others, the Novellos have thus far raised more than $40,000 toward the trawler's restoration and repair. Till recently Lena had cooked her famous spaghetti sauce and meat balls for fundraising dinners for the boat. She is the beloved mother of six children, including Sam, Joe, Peter, Vincie, Bernadette, and Grace; grandmother of 16, and great grandmother of nine.

*\*The author interviewed Lena Novello shortly before she died.*

# IN MEMORY OF LENA NOVELLO

You never forgot your roots and you made sure that no one else did by telling us stories of what it was like growing up in the Fort with all the Italians.

You cared deeply about the fishing industry and you made sure that everyone else did, too, by encouraging elected officials, community members, fishermen, and their wives to work together to maintain Gloucester's precious heritage.

You loved Saint Ann very much and you made sure that we did, too, by having us join you every July 26, her feast day, for the Crowning ceremony at Saint Ann's Church.

You loved your family very much and you made sure that they loved each other by cooking good food on your beloved stove and they shared your meals and each other's company and did not lose touch.

You translated for the immigrants, cared for the elderly and the children.

You wanted a memorial to honor the wives and families of fishermen and together we erected one.

My gratitude for our friendship.

Angela Sanfilippo

*St. Ann*

## MEATBALLS

APPROXIMATELY 25

1/3 cup garlic, minced
1 cup onion, minced
1/4 cup olive oil
2 1/2 cups bread crumbs
1 cup grated Parmesan cheese
1 teaspoon pepper
1/3 cup minced Italian parsley
4 large eggs
1/2 lb. ground pork
2 lbs. hamburger
3/4 cup water

In a skillet, heat the oil and sauté the garlic and onion. Set aside to cool.

In a bowl, combine remaining ingredients. Add garlic and onions. Form into 2" meatballs. Spray a cookie sheet with a non-stick spray. Bake at 350 degrees for 10–15 minutes.

Remember—meatballs will continue to cook in simmering sauce.

## LENA'S TOMATO SAUCE

1/2 cup olive oil
1/3 cup onion, chopped
1/4 cup garlic, minced
1 6-oz. can tomato paste
1 28-oz. can crushed tomatoes
1 tablespoon sugar
4–6 leaves fresh basil, chopped
1 can water

In a skillet, heat oil and sauté garlic and onions. Add tomato paste, crushed tomatoes, sugar, water, and basil. Mix well and simmer for 1 hour. Add meatballs and continue simmering for 1/2 hour with cover on.

*"Protecting the oceans that God has created,"* a narrative quilt created in 1998 by the members of the Gloucester Fishermen's Wives Association, tells the story of their struggles against factory trawlers, fish farming, oil drilling, and other threats to the oceans. It honors the history and faith of the fishing industry and celebrates its future. The quilt was created in conjunction with the nationally known quilt maker, Clara Wainwright. The quilt is used for educational purposes by the GFWA. On the bottom row, second panel from the right is Lena, looking out her window at the Vincie N.

## ALMOND COOKIES

MAKES 2 DOZEN

2 1/2 cups flour
2 teaspoons baking powder
2 teaspoons cinnamon
1 teaspoon ground cloves
4 cups almonds, chopped
2 eggs
1 1/2 cups dark brown sugar
1/3 cup canola oil
1/4 cup cold coffee

In a bowl, combine flour, baking powder, cinnamon, cloves, and almonds.

In a separate bowl, beat together eggs, sugar, oil, and coffee.

Add dry ingredients to creamed mixture. Let dough sit for 1 hour.

Oil hands and roll dough into two logs. Place logs on a cookie sheet lined with parchment paper. Bake at 350 degrees for 15 minutes or until done. Let cool. Cut into 1" thick slices.

## MA'S COCOA COOKIES

MAKES 3 DOZEN

4 cups flour
4 teaspoons baking powder
1/2 cup cocoa
1 cup shortening
3 eggs
1 cup sugar
1 teaspoon vanilla extract
1 cup chopped nuts

In a bowl, combine flour, baking powder, and cocoa.

In a separate bowl, beat together shortening, sugar, eggs, and vanilla.

Add dry ingredients to creamed mixture. Mix to a smooth, soft dough. Add nuts.

Form into 1" balls and place on a greased cookie sheet. Bake at 350 degrees for 10 minutes or until done. Dust with confectioners' sugar.

## PIGNULATA

SERVES 6–8

3 cups semolina flour
6 eggs, beaten
oil for frying

Glaze:
5 tablespoons honey
2 tablespoons sugar
cinnamon
1/4 cup mini chocolate chips
almonds
confectioners' sugar

Place flour in a large bowl. Make a well and add eggs. Knead until smooth. Oil hands if necessary. Let dough sit for an hour. Roll into long thin ropes and allow to sit for about an hour or until the top is hard. Cut into small pieces.

Place enough oil for frying into two separate pans. Warm oil in one pan and heat oil to high in the other pan. Begin frying by placing pignulata in warm oil. Once the pignulata has risen to the surface and turned a yellowish/white color, transfer to the hot oil. Remove when pignulata is golden brown. Repeat until all of the dough is used.

To make glaze, heat the honey and sugar in a large saucepan until it becomes bubbly. Turn heat off and add pignulata, coating each piece well. Transfer to a large platter. Garnish with cinnamon, chocolate bits, and almonds. Dust with confectioners' sugar.

*Honey coated pignulata, topped with chocolate and sugar, is a favorite Italian holiday treat.*

Every Sunday for many years Rosa Brancaleone cooked dinner for her many children and grandchildren. "It was my mother's way of getting everyone together—all of us sisters and my brother and our families and the kids with their cousins," says Rosalie Brancaleone Vitale. "The kids sat in the kitchen and the grownups in the dining room. There was a saying that as the children grew older they would graduate to the dining room. But after a while they couldn't all fit!"

"My mother always made her spaghetti and sauce, either a plain tomato sauce or a meat sauce. We'd also have beef or chicken cutlets, or baked lasagna. She might make her grey sole *pizzaiola* or fried eggplant and sauce and, in the summer, grilled eggplant fresh from the garden. After dinner there was always coffee and a sweet—one of our favorites was Philly Thumbprint Cookies; we grownups sat around the table talking over coffee and cookies while the kids played."

"My mother never measured anything—even when she was baking. She'd put in a little of this and a little of that by the feel of the hand. I'm the same way," says Rosalie. "If someone asks me for a recipe, I have to start from scratch; I have to weigh and measure everything and then test the recipe."

Nowadays Rosalie Vitale does Sunday dinner at her house for own her children and grandchildren. Her mother, Rosa, a hale 88-year-old, attends when she's in Gloucester; the older woman now lives with Rosalie and her husband, Leo, but spends the colder months with her other children who live in Florida, California, and Texas.

To a younger generation of Sicilian-Americans,

"Rosa Brancaleone has been everyone's nonna in America," says Angela Sanfilippo, a close family friend. Angela's and Rosalie's families have been close since the two were young children in Sicily; in fact, the Brancaleones encouraged Angela's parents to move to Gloucester. When Angela got married, she remembers, "Rosa ironed my trousseau, sheets, nightgowns, everything. After my brother Vince was born she came and helped my mother give him a bath."

Rosalie remembers, "for a while Angela's family lived downstairs from us. Her mother, Antonina, a seamstress, sewed clothes for me and my baby daughter. We often had dinner together. We were like one big family."

A tall, graceful, and well-spoken woman, Rosalie landed in Gloucester, from Terrasini, Sicily, in 1956 at age 11. She came with her mother, her older brother, Tom, and her four younger sisters. Rosalie's father, Francesco Paolo Brancaleone, a Terrasini city councilor and a lifelong fishermen, had arrived a couple of years earlier and was already fishing here with his brother and nephews.

Because she was not fluent in English, Rosalie was placed in a class with students several years younger, a frustrating situation aggravated by the fact that she was tall. She quit high school and age 16 and studied hairdressing. She worked as a hairdresser through the births of her first two children.

Rosalie and Leo had four children. Their youngest, Franceso Paul, 32, a graduate of Massachusetts Maritime Academy, now fishes with his father aboard the *Angela and Rose*. Rosalie and Leo's oldest child, Nick, 39, lives and works in California; their daughter, Rose, 34, works for Fidelity in Boston. Rosalie and

*Rosalie, along with other fishermen's wives, at the Tavern on the Harbor, Gloucester, with Senator Ted Kennedy in 1981.*

Leo have two grandchildren and one other on its way.

Twelve years ago, their daughter, Angela, suffered a broken engagement and committed suicide, a tragedy felt not only by their family, but the entire community. Friends and family in Gloucester, Italy, everywhere lent comfort and support, doing all they could to extend their love in the face of terrible loss. "Everyone was so good to us," says Rosalie.

Rosalie is the longtime treasurer of the Gloucester Fishermen's Wives Association. She's been active in the organization for a quarter century, traveling to Washington, D.C., twice, once to support Angela Sanfilippo who was testifying before Congress, and another time to take part in a salute to the organization at the Smithsonian Institution, where Rosalie and several other Wives demonstrated various ways to cook Cape shark (dogfish) and herring. Over the years, Rosalie has also cooked and served fish at the Boston Seafood Show and numerous seafood festivals and benefits.

## PASTA WITH FAVA BEAN SAUCE
SERVES 4

1/2 cup olive oil
1 1/2 cups onion, chopped
1 garlic clove, peeled and minced
1 1/2 cups shelled fresh small fava beans (about 2 lbs. in the shell)
1/2 cup fresh parsley, chopped
1 cup water
1 teaspoon salt
1 lb. rigatoni

In a skillet, heat oil on low heat and sauté onions and garlic until soft.

Add fava beans, half of the parsley, and water. Cover pan and cook over medium heat for 10 minutes or until beans are tender. Remove pan from heat, add salt to taste, and set aside.

Cook rigatoni according to package directions until al dente. Drain.

Pour half of the sauce into a large serving bowl. Add rigatoni and toss. Pour the remaining sauce on top and sprinkle with remaining parsley. Serve immediately.

## SWISS CHICKEN CUTLETS
SERVES 8

4 thin slices reduced-fat Swiss cheese
8 chicken cutlets (4 ounces each), 1/4" thick
4 tablespoons all purpose flour
1 teaspoon pepper
2 tablespoons unsalted butter or margarine
1 cup reduced sodium chicken broth
1/2 cup dry white wine or chicken broth
1/2 teaspoon dried oregano
chopped fresh parsley and oregano for garnish

Dredge cutlets in flour. Cut each cheese slice in half. Place on top of each cutlet. Starting with a short end, tightly roll up cutlets, and secure with one or two toothpicks.

In a large non-stick skillet, melt butter over medium heat and add the rolled-up cutlets. Cook, turning frequently until golden brown (about 3 minutes).

Add broth, wine, and oregano to skillet. Increase heat and bring to a boil. Reduce heat to medium-low and simmer until chicken is cooked and sauce has slightly thickened (about 10–12 minutes).

Place on platter. Garnish with parsley and oregano.

## GREY SOLE PIZZAIOLA
**(Grey Sole Pizza Style)**
SERVES 6–8

2 lbs. grey sole fillets
1 cup Italian seasoned bread crumbs
1 28-oz. can crushed peeled tomatoes
1/2 can water
1 cup onion, minced
1/4 cup oregano
3/4 cup olive oil, divided
1/4 cup grated Romano cheese
salt and pepper to taste

Sauté onion in 1/3 cup of olive oil until golden brown and softened. Add tomatoes and water and simmer on medium-low heat, stirring frequently for 30 minutes.

Place remaining olive oil in a bowl. Dip fish in oil and then into bread crumbs. Arrange fish in a single layer on a 12" x 18" greased baking tray (spray with a non-stick spray). Cover fish with tomato sauce. Sprinkle oregano and cheese on top. Bake at 350 degrees for 25 minutes, uncovered.

## EGGPLANT AND TOMATO CASSEROLE
SERVES 6-8

2 medium eggplants (about 2 1/2 lbs.)
2 cups boiling water
salt and pepper to taste
1/2 cup salad oil
2 garlic cloves, finely chopped
2 tablespoons flour
2 1-lb. cans stewed tomatoes, undrained
2 teaspoons sugar
1 teaspoon paprika
1/8 teaspoon dried basil leaves
1/2 cup grated Parmesan cheese

Wash and pare eggplant. Cut into 2" cubes. Place eggplant in a saucepan. Cover with water and a dash of salt. Simmer for 10 minutes and drain.

Heat oil in a skillet and sauté onions until golden.

Stir in flour, tomatoes, sugar, paprika, pepper, and basil. Cook, stirring over medium heat, until mixture boils and has thickened.

Lightly grease a small casserole dish. Layer eggplant cubes, alternating with tomato mixture. Top with grated cheese. Bake at 375 degrees for 5 minutes or until lightly brown.

## PHILLY THUMBPRINT COOKIES
MAKES 3 DOZEN

1 1/2 cups butter
1 1/2 cups sugar
8 oz. cream cheese
2 eggs
2 teaspoons lemon juice
1 1/2 teaspoons lemon rind
4 1/2 cups flour
1 1/2 teaspoons baking powder

In a bowl, combine all ingredients. Refrigerate for 1 hour. Form mixture into balls and place on a greased cookie sheet. Make a thumbprint on each ball. Top with a little jam (apricot, apple, or strawberry). Bake at 350 degrees for 15 minutes. When done, sprinkle with confectioners' sugar.

## ORANGE RAISIN MUFFINS
MAKES 1 DOZEN

1 orange, cut into quarters (peel included)
1/2 cup raisins or dates
1/2 cup skim milk
1/4 cup canola oil
1 egg
1 1/2 cups all purpose flour
1/3 cup Equal sweetener
1 teaspoon baking soda
1 teaspoon baking powder
pinch of salt

In a blender or food processor, combine orange, raisins, milk, oil, and egg. Process for 10 seconds or until orange and raisins are chopped. In a bowl, combine flour, Equal, baking soda, baking powder, and salt. Pour contents of blender into flour mixture. Stir until mixed. Spoon into lightly greased non-stick muffin pans, filling 3/4 full. Bake at 400 degrees for 20–25 minutes or until golden brown.

"Go back to the kitchen where you belong!" To 42-year old Sefatia Giambanco Romeo, a cook, fisherman's wife, and lifelong activist, those are fighting words.

"I'm in the kitchen because I choose to be," says Sefatia. She regularly prepares, among other dishes, fish and clam chowders for her family; fried and baked fish and sweet and sour hors d'oeuvres for Gloucester's Seafood and New Fish Festivals, and lasagna, for 350 persons, during St. Peter's Fiesta. She served herring burgers to a dozen top Boston chefs during a reception at the Boston Harbor Hotel. The reception culminated a year-long Gloucester Fishermen's Wives Association project involving the development and marketing of various herring products.

If cooking is Sefatia's passion, advocacy is her calling. An award winning community health liaison for Addison Gilbert Hospital and a respected Gloucester City Councilor, she is a fearless ally of all those who might otherwise have no voice—senior citizens, children, those who are ill, jobless, without adequate food, housing, or medical coverage. "I live and breathe for peoples' rights," says Sefatia. "This is not a job to me, this is life."

In 1998 Sefatia received Health Care for All's prestigious "People Against the Tide" award along with commendations from federal, state, and local officials. A longtime vice-president of the GFWA, she worked closely with the organization to help lay the groundwork for the first subsidized health plan for US fishermen.

While fiercely compassionate, Sefatia can also be tough. She has stood her ground when fishermen, dis-gruntled over new regulations, have shouted at her, "go back to the kitchen." She has told them: "you have a choice": either work with those trying to save the fish and fishing industry "or be left behind."

Besides marrying into a Sicilian-American fishing family, Sefatia grew up in one. Her grandfather and uncles all fished. "When the men were home, it was like a party; there was always plenty of fish, conversation, and laughter." When they were at sea, Sefatia stayed at her grandmother's. She enjoyed this ritual, except during electrical storms; then the old woman turned out the lights, clutched Sefatia and her rosary, reciting the verses as thunder shook the house and lightening streaked the sky.

Sefatia's childhood home, at the corner of Church and Middle Streets, looks out onto several churches. Twenty years ago while sitting on the porch with her mother, Sefatia first met the GFWA's president, Angela Sanfilippo.

"I heard women speaking Italian, looked up and recognized Angela from the newspaper. She was carrying, as usual, tons and tons of bags. I asked if she needed help." The Association then held meetings at St. John's Church. Sefatia met some of the Wives, who were setting out coffee and home-baked cookies—the sustenance of any GFWA gathering. Over the next years, Angela took the younger woman under her wing.

Sefatia's husband, Nino, was fishing and she was raising their three daughters, Carla, now 23, Lia, 21, and Melissa, 19, while also taking care of her ailing in-laws. Like many fishing families, the senior Romeos lacked medical insurance. When Mrs. Romeo was diagnosed with ovarian cancer, Sefatia did everything she could, including translating: she negotiated with doctors and with various federal, state, and volunteer agencies—she even wound up training a home health aide. By age 23 Sefatia was on her way to becoming a grass-roots health care advocate.

Her father, Enzo Giambanco, had done much the same thing all of his life. He was a smart, charming, and charismatic man with a zeal for social justice, yet he could be difficult. Sefatia was the only one in the family who dared challenge him, possibly because she was the most like him.

"My brother, Anthony, inherited my father's looks and charisma; my sister Marianne inherited his organizational skills, my sister Rosaria, the way he loved to dress, and Grace, a little of both. I took his anger, his political life, his advocacy, and temper. I also inherited his mouth. My father never kept his mouth shut. I'm the same way."

Enzo Giambanco died in 1977, when Sefatia was only 15. Despite his considerable successes helping others, he endured a long battle against lung cancer without medical coverage because of a practice, since outlawed, which barred coverage for "pre-existing conditions." After his death, Sefatia's mother faced massive hospital bills, which "cleaned out her entire savings." Sefatia did not discover this until some years later, partly because her mother sought to protect her.

Sefatia's mother, the former Rosalia Cilluffo, was "the quiet, strong type." A nurturing and uncomplaining woman, she was also "an awesome cook. My father brought everyone you could think of over. My mother was always in the kitchen while he was advocating and hosting. Everyone loved her linguine and white clam sauce and her fish soup. You can't even make my mother's meat balls and sauce!"

Rosalia worked her entire life cutting and packing fish—for O'Donnell-Usen, Kennebec, and Gorton-Pew. She tried to prevent her daughters from following in her footsteps. She cried when, in 1986 Sefatia applied for a job at Gorton's. Nino had just lost his boat and Sefatia needed to support the family. The job was every bit as tough as Rosalia had predicted:

"eight hours on the line packing fish with only a half-hour lunch break and two 15-minute coffee breaks. You had to ask permission to go to the bathroom. Standing on the cement floor with cold air freezers blowing at you, the women developed varicose veins, arthritis, backaches, repetitive strain injury."

Sefatia survived her four years as a fish packer partly because she knew, "it was only temporary." She helped translate and advocate for her fellow packers at contract time, formed lasting friendships, and became accepted as "one of the Gorton's girls."

"The job helped me grow. It made me stronger, and made me appreciate the work that others do," says Sefatia.

Today, as a health care advocate and city councilor, Sefatia continues to speak out against injustice, while also fighting "to unlock hidden doors." Her anger has been tempered at least partly by her own suffering, particularly by the deaths of her "two best friends," her husband, in 1997, and her mother, the following year.

"I'm not Joan of Arc and I'm not going to change the world" says Sefatia. "I have a lot of different clients. I bond with them because, unfortunately, I've walked in so many shoes: I've been rich, I've been poor, I've been overweight, I've been thin. I've helped people with addiction, mental depression, all kinds of problems. I don't want to change people. I just want them to wake up."

Sefatia's father named her after an Egyptian queen. When she was an infant he predicted: "You are going to be a strong, strong person. I can see from the way you fight and kick and the way those big eyes look that you are going to accomplish a lot and use your voice." Besides three daughters, Sefatia has a grandson, A. J.

Sefatia speaks truth to power, and undoubtedly always will.

## MAMA LIA'S BASIC COOKIE RECIPE WITH SUGAR ICING
### (best in "S" shape or braided)
MAKES 3–4 DOZEN

4 eggs
1 tablespoon vanilla
5 cups flour
1 1/2 cups sugar
5 teaspoons baking powder
5 heaping tablespoons shortening
1/2 cup milk

Icing: 1 lb. confectioners' sugar and approximately 1/4 cup milk

In a bowl, beat eggs and vanilla. Set aside.

Mix all dry ingredients (flour, sugar, and baking powder). Slowly work shortening into dry ingredients using your hands.

Dough will be crumbly. Add egg mixture (still using your hands).

Slowly add milk until dough forms (only add as much milk as necessary to form dough).

Roll out dough, cut it, and then shape it into an S or a braid.

Bake at 400 degrees for 10 minutes.

Let cookies cool for 5 minutes.

Icing: slowly add milk to confectioners' sugar. Beat until creamy. Spread icing on cookies using your fingers. Store in a sealed container.

## LIA'S BANANA SPLIT CHEESECAKE
MAKES 12–15 SERVINGS

2 cups graham cracker crumbs
1/2 cup margarine, melted
1 cup butter, softened
8 oz. cream cheese, softened
1 1/2 cups confectioners' sugar
1 teaspoon almond extract
4 bananas
19-oz. can crushed pineapple, drained
2 cups whipping cream, graham cracker crumbs, nuts

In a bowl, combine the graham cracker crumbs and margarine. Press into 9" x 13" pan. Bake at 350 degrees for 10 minutes. Cool.

In a mixing bowl, combine butter, cream cheese, confectioners' sugar, and almond extract. Beat until smooth. Spread over cooled base. Refrigerate until firm.

Slice bananas lengthwise. Layer bananas over cream cheese mixture. Spread crushed pineapple over bananas.

Top with whipped cream. Garnish with wafer crumbs or nuts.

Refrigerate until ready to serve.

*Mama Lia's Basic Cookie Recipe can be used to create these traditional Pupu Cu L'ova (Easter Basket cookies).*

## BANANA MUFFINS
MAKES 24 MUFFINS

2/3 cup vegetable oil
1 cup sugar
2 eggs
2 ripe bananas, mashed
2 cups flour
1 teaspoon baking soda
1/2 teaspoon salt
1 teaspoon cinnamon
1/2 cup buttermilk

In a small mixing bowl, beat oil, sugar, eggs, and mashed bananas.

In a large mixing bowl, combine flour, baking soda, salt, and cinnamon. Add the oil mixture and buttermilk. Mix well.

Fill muffin tins 2/3 full and bake at 375 degrees for about 20 minutes.

You may also add chocolate chips or walnuts.

## CHILI WITH MEAT
SERVES 6–8

2 tablespoons vegetable oil
1 1/2 lbs. lean ground beef
1 cup onion, chopped
2 garlic cloves, minced
2 cups stewed tomatoes
1 cup crushed tomatoes
2 14-oz. cans kidney beans
14 oz. can pork and beans
1 teaspoon hot chili or pepper

Heat oil in a large skillet and sauté beef, onion, and garlic until beef is no longer pink.

Add remaining ingredients. Simmer for 1 hour, stirring occasionally.

Serve hot.

## MATZA'S LASAGNA
SERVES 6–8

1 12-oz. package lasagna noodles
1 1/2 lbs. ground beef
1 cup onion, chopped
1 28-oz. can tomato sauce
1/2 can water
2 garlic cloves, crushed
1 teaspoon basil, crushed
2 cups ricotta cheese
1/2 cup Parmesan cheese
1 egg, beaten
12 oz. mozzarella cheese

Cook noodles according to package directions. Rinse and set aside.

In a skillet, sauté onions with beef until beef is cooked. Add tomato sauce, water, garlic, and crushed basil. Simmer for 15 minutes. Set aside. In a separate bowl, combine ricotta cheese, Parmesan cheese, and egg.

Lightly grease a 9" x 13" lasagna dish. Place a layer of noodles in dish. Then layer half of the meat mixture, another layer of noodles, the entire cheese mixture, another layer of noodles, and the other half of the meat mixture. Place mozzarella on top.

Cover with foil and bake at 375 degrees for about 40 minutes. Uncover and bake for another 15 minutes.

## SICILIAN SALAD
SERVES 6–8

6 ripe tomatoes, thickly sliced
1 1/4 lbs. mozzarella cheese, thickly sliced
8–10 fresh basil leaves, coarsely chopped
1/4 cup extra virgin olive oil/ red wine vinegar (optional)
salt and pepper to taste

On a large serving plate, alternate tomatoes and mozzarella slices. Sprinkle with basil and salt and pepper, and drizzle with vinegar and olive oil.


## PAPA'S LINGUINE WITH SEAFOOD SAUCE
SERVES 6

2 tablespoons margarine
1/2 cup white onions, chopped
3 garlic cloves, minced
4 oz. medium shrimp
4 oz. scallops
2 tablespoons lemon juice
1 cup chicken broth
1/2 cup white wine (dry)
1/2 teaspoon hot pepper (optional)
2 teaspoons cornstarch
2 tablespoons water
12 oz. linguine pasta
1/4 cup light sour cream
2 tablespoons margarine

In a skillet, melt margarine. Add onions and garlic and sauté.

Stir in the shrimp, scallops, lemon juice, chicken broth, and wine. Heat to boiling. Reduce heat and simmer for 5 minutes

Combine the cornstarch with the water and add to seafood mixture. Stir until sauce thickens. Keep warm.

Meanwhile, cook the linguine according to package directions. Drain. Rinse with hot water. Toss linguine with sour cream and margarine.

Spoon into a large pasta bowl. Spoon seafood sauce on top.

Garnish with lemon wedges and fresh parsley.


## SPINACH DELUXE

10-oz. package frozen chopped spinach, thawed and drained
4-oz. package stuffing with seasonings
3 eggs, well beaten
1 medium onion, chopped
1/2 cup butter, melted
1/2 cup grated Parmesan cheese
1/2 teaspoon garlic powder
1/2 teaspoon salt

In a large mixing bowl, combine all ingredients.

Spread mixture in a greased 1 1/2 quart baking dish.

Bake at 350 degrees for 15 minutes or until top is crusty.


## HAM 'N CHEESE QUICHE
SERVES 5–6

1 9" unbaked pie shell
1 1/2 cups cooked ham, cubed
2 cups grated mozzarella cheese
3 eggs
2 onions, chopped
1/4 teaspoon salt
1 cup milk
2 tablespoons grated Parmesan cheese

Distribute the ham and cheese evenly in the pie shell.

In a small bowl, beat eggs, salt, and milk. Add onions. Pour over ham and cheese.

Sprinkle with Parmesan cheese.

Bake at 375 degrees for 30–35 minutes.

You may use Swiss cheese instead of mozzarella.

## MAMA'S FISH CHOWDER

SERVES 6

2 lbs. white fish fillets
2 tablespoons butter
1 cup chopped onion
1/2 cup diced celery
3 cups diced raw potatoes
3 cups water
1 teaspoon salt
1/4 teaspoon pepper
2 cups milk

Cut fillets into bite sized pieces.

In a large saucepan, melt butter. Sauté the onions and celery in the butter until tender. Add potatoes, water, and salt and pepper. Simmer until vegetables are tender (about 20 min).

Add fish and cook at low-medium heat for about 10 minutes. Add milk and reheat (but do not boil).

## MANHATTAN CLAM CHOWDER

SERVES 5

4 bacon slices, chopped
1 large onion, chopped
1/2 cup celery, chopped
2 cups water
2 cups potatoes, peeled and diced
2 teaspoons salt
1/2 teaspoon pepper
2  8-oz. cans crushed tomatoes
2 10-oz. cans clams

In a large, heavy saucepan, cook bacon. Drain most of the fat. Add onions and celery. Cook until onions are translucent.

Add remaining ingredients, except for clams.

Simmer gently for 1 to 2 hours, or until vegetables are tender. Add clams during the last 10 minutes of cooking. Serve hot.

## CHEDDAR N' GARLIC LOAF

SERVES 6–8

1 loaf French bread
3/4 cup butter
2 cups grated cheddar cheese
1/4 cup sour cream
3 garlic cloves, crushed
1 tablespoon fresh parsley, chopped

Slice the French bread in half lengthwise and place on a cookie sheet.

In a bowl, combine remaining ingredients. Mix well.

Spread cheese mixture over the 2 halves of bread.

Bake at 350 degrees for 12 minutes, or until bubbly. Slice and serve warm.

## BRUSCHETTA

MAKES 4 SLICES

4 thick slices Italian bread
2 tablespoons olive oil
1 small garlic clove, minced
1 large tomato, diced
1 scallion, chopped
2 teaspoons fresh basil, chopped
1/4 teaspoon ground pepper
2 oz. grated mozzarella cheese and Romano cheese

In a bowl, combine oil and garlic. Brush mixture onto bread slices and place on a cookie sheet.

In a separate bowl, combine tomato, scallion, basil, and pepper. Spoon over bread slices. Sprinkle cheese on top.

Bake at 450 degrees for about 5 minutes or until bubbly.

*The Greasy Pole competition is one of the highlights of the St. Peter's Fiesta. Participants try to retrieve a flag nailed to the end of a 35' pole that is covered with industrial grease.*

Photo courtesy of Desi Smith

## LIA'S CLAM CHOWDER

SERVES 6

5 slices bacon, chopped
1 medium onion, chopped
1 celery heart, chopped
2 10-oz. cans clams, chopped
3 cups potatoes, cubed
2 cups water
1 teaspoon salt
1/2 teaspoon pepper
1/4 teaspoon thyme
2 tablespoons butter
2 tablespoons flour
2 cups heavy cream

In a large pan, fry bacon. Drain bacon fat (all but 1 tablespoon). Add onions and celery and sauté until tender. Add potatoes, water, salt, and thyme. Cook for 15-20 minutes.

Add clams and clam juice.

In a separate pan, melt butter. Add enough flour to make a paste. Slowly wisk in heavy cream. Add the potatoes and bring to a boil. Turn heat down and simmer for 10 minutes.

## NONNA'S LINGUINE WITH RED CLAM SAUCE

SERVES 4

8 oz. linguine pasta
2 10-oz. cans baby clams
2 tablespoons butter
2 garlic cloves, minced (more if desired)
1/2 cup white onions, chopped
1 28-oz. can crushed tomatoes
1 cup white wine
1 teaspoon salt
1/2 teaspoon pepper

Cook linguine according to package directions.

Meanwhile, drain clams, reserving liquid.

In a skillet, heat butter and sauté clams, garlic, and onions for 5 minutes.

Add reserved clam juice, tomatoes, and white wine. Stir well. Bring to a boil, reduce heat, and simmer for 20 minutes. Add salt and pepper.

Serve linguine topped with clam sauce.

## LIA'S BEEF STEW

SERVES 6

1/4 cup flour
1 teaspoon salt
1/2 teaspoon pepper
1 1/2 lbs. stewing beef, cubed
1/4 cup vegetable oil
2 medium onions, sliced
1 garlic clove, minced
1/2 teaspoon thyme
2 bay leaves
1 16-oz. can diced tomatoes
2 cups water
4 carrots, peeled and sliced
3 potatoes, peeled and diced
3 celery stalks, chopped

In a large pan, heat oil. Add beef cubes and brown. Add onion, garlic, thyme, and bay leaves. Cook at low-medium heat for 1 hour.

Add remaining ingredients and continue to simmer until tender. Remove bay leaves.

Add water and flour to thicken, as desired.

## NONNA'S SPAGHETTI SAUCE

SERVES 6–8

2 tablespoons olive oil
1 medium onion, chopped
3 garlic cloves, minced
2 28-oz. cans crushed tomatoes
1 can water
1 teaspoon salt
1/2 teaspoon pepper
2 tablespoons sugar
3 basil leaves

In a large pan, heat oil and sauté onions and garlic.

Add both cans of tomatoes and water. Cook on medium heat for about 15 minutes.

Add salt, pepper, and sugar. Simmer for about 20 minutes.

Add basil leaves and simmer for another 15 minutes. Serve with spaghetti.

(Meatballs optional)

## AJ'S MEATBALLS

SERVES 6–8

2 lbs. lean ground beef
1 cup bread crumbs
1/4 cup milk
1 egg
1 teaspoon salt
1/2 teaspoon pepper
1/2 teaspoon garlic powder or 4 garlic cloves, chopped
1/2 teaspoon onion powder
1/4 cup grated Romano cheese

In a bowl, combine all ingredients and mix well.

Roll into 2" balls (smaller or bigger as desired).

Place on a baking pan and bake at 450 degrees for 30–40 minutes or until done.

Put meatballs in Nonna's sauce and continue cooking for another 30–40 minutes.

The Grand Isle, *whose home port is Gloucester.*

The sweet smells of *cucciddata*, Christmas fig cookies, baking in wood-fired ovens flooded the streets of Nina Groppo's hometown and animate her stories of Sicilian village life. She laughs when she remembers dipping a naughty finger into a sugary glaze ("we kids loved it!") while her grandmother and a neighbor lifted huge trays of *cucciddata* into the brick oven. And ask her about her Aunt Rusidda's *surrogato di caffè*, a coffee and barley drink brewed with a cinnamon stick. "You have to taste it!" she exclaims, clapping her hands.

Nina's enthusiasm for cooking, eating, (and living) are contagious! A youthful 47-year-old mother, grandmother, and fisherman's wife, Nina is as smart as she is energetic—and multilingual. Nina grew up in Trappeto, a Sicilian farming and fishing town of 3,500, in an era when residents still baked together in the brick ovens, shined pots together, and sat around a brazier at night talking, crocheting, and reading. "It would be winter, raining, and cold and someone would say, 'Mastro Luigino is roasting chestnuts.' You could smell them all over town. We kids would go out and buy everyone a cone."

"And the holidays! Holidays in our little towns were the best!" Christmas preparations began in early December. Nina's family and others got together then to bake big batches of *cucciddata*, also called *buccellati*. ("We're not talking one or two kilos, but ten or more!") At Easter she and her grandmother made *pupu cu l'ova* (see picture on page 76); they'd form cookie dough into the shape of a bunny, a basket or even a heart and place a colored hardboiled egg in the middle. "I still make them today; if I don't my kids remind me that something is missing." On *I Morti*,

All Soul's Day, when traditionally Sicilian children received their holiday presents (rather than at Christmas), people throughout the villages eat a light crunchy cookie called *nucatoli* or *ossa di morti* (bones of the dead). On 11 November, they serve *biscotti di San Martino*, a hard anise-flavored cookie, dipped in new wine to mark the feast of that saint.

Today Nina prepares many of the foods she loved as a child, including *pasta al forno* and *sfinciuni*, a deep dish pizza traditionally served in Trappeto on the occasion of enclosing a house as a symbol of good luck. While many dishes are associated with religious and other celebrations, "mostly we ate very simple foods," says Nina. "Pasta with *fagioli*, pasta with *cucuzza* and *tenerumi* (Sicilian zucchini and leaves), pasta with peas and favas—all freshly-picked because my grandfather was a farmer. We made snail and fish soups, and *bruschetta*. That was fun! We'd get the frying pan hot and drizzle the bread with oil and sprinkle a little salt and pepper." Nina made her first *manicotti* at age eight, in a small, round, electric oven, which her parents sent her from Germany.

Vincenza and Matteo Cusumano, had left Trappeto to find factory work in 1960 when Nina, an only child, was three. She joined them in Ohligs, Germany, in 1968, following the earthquake in Sicily. She attended school in Germany for three years, leaving at age 15 to work at the Nägle scissors factory, across from her house. Nina was a good worker, a fast worker, who refused to be intimidated by a supervisor who verbally abused his crew. The day he lashed out at Nina, she spoke up: "Nobody talks to me that way." She burst out crying and quit. She immediately found other factory work, keeping busy till she heard from Nägle colleagues that her old supervisor wanted to talk to her. He offered her a job at double the rate she had been making elsewhere and promised to hold his tongue. "You cannot imagine the change in this guy, not just toward me, but everybody." When the women in his department went on strike, Nina's supervisor went out with them. He said, "if my girls are going, I'm going too!"

From Germany, Nina secretly corresponded with her beloved, Franco Groppo, in Trappeto. She sent letters to his cousin and he to her friend in Germany. There was no opportunity to date (her grandmother was very strict) but they became engaged, with the blessing of both sets of parents, when she was 16 and he 20. They married in Trappeto in July 1976, and moved to Gloucester soon after. When Nina arrived she did not speak English; she learned quickly from watching Sesame Street with Maria, their first child, born in 1977. Vincenza (Enza) was born in 1982.

When Maria was four-months old, Nina got a job packing fish at Gorton's. She shared childcare with her sister-in-law, Maria, also a Gorton's employee. Maria worked the morning shift, and Nina, at night. "I'd pick up the baby from my sister-in-law's late at night; that was really tough, especially in the winter. I wasn't yet driving." At Franco's urging, Nina quit. She took adult education courses, including one that trained her to be a travel agent. In the years that followed she worked in travel, in a law office, and as a translator, among other jobs. She has also taught Italian. In 1982 and again in 1993, she became the sole breadwinner, when Franco suffered injuries on the boat. In 1994, Nina took a job at the then new Gloucester Fisherman and Family Assistance Center, where she works today as a bilingual employment and training counselor.

Franco shares Nina's appreciation for good food and he, too, is a skilled cook, having honed his culinary expertise while working aboard Gloucester fishing boats. Today he prepares, among other dishes, *pasta carrettiera* (pasta with fresh tomatoes, garlic, and basil) and *sogliola in bianco* (poached sole with lemon

*Nina, age 2.*

and garlic) for his crewmates aboard the groundfish dragger, *Miss Trish II.*

In Gloucester Nina and Franco bring alive the spirit of a Sicilian village on the feast day of San Giuseppe. The celebration concludes a nine-day novena in which Nina and others recite the rosary and sing. Nina first offered the novena nine years ago, to give thanks for her mother's health. Nowadays, on the eve of the feast, a priest celebrates mass for more than 100 people, relatives and friends, who pack the Groppo's modest house. Each person goes home with a small bag containing an orange, signifying the sweetness of life, a lemon, the bitterness, and St. Joseph's bread, the sustenance. The following day, Nina serves more than 80 pounds of the ritual St. Joseph's pasta, made with fresh *tagliarini* and the traditional *conza* or sauce consisting of a mix of beans,

*The feast of St. Joseph is celebrated each year on the 19th of March. Ornate altars are created in homes throughout Gloucester in honor of St. Joseph. During this celebration, visitors partake in prayer, and enjoy many dishes prepared especially for the occasion. Pictured here is Nina's St. Joseph's alter.*

chick peas, lentils, cauliflower, celery, carrots, and wild fennel.

Nina and six to eight women friends make the *tagliarini*, a flat wide pasta similar to *fettucine*. The night before Franco and several other men mix the dough. They meet at a friend's restaurant after closing and use the large, industrial, mixer. Filippo, who grew up in a family of bakers, oversees the operation. "He knows how many eggs, how much semolina flour, how much water, and the consistency."

Nina's crew usually starts at 8 AM. "We have our coffee and a little breakfast then set up in the garage." Nina's garage functions as a second kitchen. "One woman rolls the dough, another cuts it and pats it square, another passes it through the machine to make the *tagliarini*. Another puts it on tables to dry. When we're done we have five or six tables full of pasta!"

The morning of the feast, everyone pitches in. There are, among others, sun dried tomatoes to be stuffed, squid and octopus salad to be made. And *i dolci: sfinci*—the traditional deep fried fritters, which the cooks prepare with rice, and *cassateddi*, turnovers, which they stuff with a sweet chickpea filling, then deep fry, and roll in cinnamon and sugar. Also *zeppole di San Giuseppe*, that luscious confection made with sweet ricotta cream.

"By reciting the rosary, making the pasta, being part of the celebration, people in their own ways are expressing their intentions," says Nina. Besides, she says, "its fun. We work hard. We laugh. We eat. And you know, it feels good. Everybody comes together; it's a nice way to say thank you for all the things we are fortunate to have."

In the winter of 2003–04, Nina appeared for the Gloucester Fishermen's Wives Association as a guest on the Food Network's "Sara's Secrets." A longtime member of the association, she talked about being a fisherman's wife and demonstrated how to prepare old-fashioned baked stuffed squid.

You cannot visit Nina without being offered at the very least a cup of strong espresso and a platter of freshly-baked *dolci*. "Mangia! Mangia!" she insists.

## SAVORY PEAS, MUSHROOMS AND ARTICHOKES
SERVES 3–4

6 fresh artichokes hearts, cut in half or 1 package
frozen artichoke hearts
1 lb. sweet baby peas
1 large onion, sliced
1 16-oz. package porcini mushrooms
1/4 lb. prosciutto cotto or ham, coarsely chopped
4 tablespoons olive oil
6 sprigs parsley, chopped
1/2 cup wine
1/4 cup water
salt and pepper to taste
6 eggs (optional)

Place peas, artichokes hearts, and oil in a large skillet. Add the prosciutto, onion, mushrooms, and salt and pepper. Stir fry, adding the wine and water.

Cover and cook for about 1/2 hour. At this point, adjust the taste by adding salt and pepper. Cook over high heat to absorb excess liquid.

Add parsley and serve as a side dish.

If serving as a main dish, keep excess liquid. Break in the eggs. Cover and reduce heat. When eggs are veiled in white (approx. 5 minutes), they are ready to serve. Serve with Italian bread.

## PASTA WITH CUCUZZA
**Nonna Nzina's way**
SERVES 3–4

6 cups water
1 Sicilian zucchini (or 2 large summer
zucchinis), cubed
1 cup ditalini or spaghetti, broken into little pieces

2 teaspoons salt or to taste
1/4 cup oil
1 tablespoon butter
1 egg, slightly beaten
1–2 tablespoons grated Romano cheese

Bring water and salt to a boil in a 4-quart saucepan. Add the zucchini and cook for about 10 minutes.

Add the pasta and cook for 15 miinutes. Drain some of the excess water from the pan, reserving 1 cup, but still leaving it very soupy. Add the oil and butter and bring to a boil. Remove from heat.

In a small bowl, beat the egg and add the grated cheese. Add this to the pasta. Stir well. Cook for 2 minutes.

Add the reserved water if the pasta seems dry. Serve with grated cheese.

## POLPETTINE DI MOLLICA

3 eggs
1/2 cup seasoned bread crumbs
2 tablespoons milk
2 tablespoons grated Romano cheese
2 sprigs parsley, chopped
2 basil leaves, chopped
oil for frying

Beat the eggs with the milk for a couple of minutes. Add dry ingredients and mix well. Mixture should be soft.

Using a teaspoon, drop the mixture into oil and fry until golden brown. Serve plain or add to your favorite tomato sauce instead of meatballs.

## CHICKEN MEATBALLS WITH ROMAINE LETTUCE SOUP

SERVES 6

For the chicken meatballs:
1 lb. ground chicken
1 egg
1/2 cup grated Romano (or Parmesan) cheese
4–5 sprigs parsley, chopped
2–3 leaves basil, chopped
1 garlic clove, crushed
1/2 cup flavored bread crumbs
salt and pepper to taste
1/4 cup white wine (can substitute with water or milk)

For the soup:
2 hearts romaine lettuce
8 cups water
1/4 cup olive oil
1 medium onion, chopped
1 chicken bouillon cube

To prepare chicken meatballs:
In a bowl, use your hands to combine ground chicken, egg, cheese, parsley, basil, bread crumbs, garlic, salt and pepper, and wine. Mixture should be soft. Add more bread crumbs or wine if needed. Shape into little balls and set aside.

To prepare soup:
Thoroughly wash and clean the lettuce and cut it into pieces. In a 6-quart saucepan, sauté onion in oil until translucent. Add lettuce and salt and pepper. Sauté for a couple of minutes and add water and bouillon. Stir and let cook until lettuce becomes wilted.

Add the chicken meatballs. Stir gently to mix all ingredients in pan. Cover and cook on medium heat until the meatballs are done (about 15–20 minutes depending on the size). Taste and adjust flavor with salt and pepper.

Add a heaping tablespoon of your favorite grated cheese and serve.

Note: The ingredients for the chicken meatballs recipe can also be used to make turkey balls or meatballs. All three types can be added to tomato sauce. For the health conscious, when making meatballs, instead of frying, bake them in your oven at 450 degrees, then add to your favorite sauce.

## FRICASSEA DI POLLO

SERVES 4

1 lb. chicken pieces, thighs, breasts, drumsticks
2 tablespoons flour
1 large onion, quartered
1 8-oz. package porcini mushrooms
1 package frozen artichoke hearts
1 package frozen baby peas
4 tablespoons olive oil
salt and pepper
parsley
1 cup white wine

Wash and dry chicken. Season with salt and pepper and coat with flour. Heat oil in a large skillet and sear the chicken until golden on both sides.

Leaving the chicken in the skillet, add onion, mushrooms, artichokes, peas, wine, and a little salt and pepper to taste. Cover and cook on medium heat for about 30 minutes or until cooked. Sprinkle with parsley and serve.

Great with boiled baby potatoes or mashed potatoes.

Note: Turkey or pork can also be used for this recipe.

*Fricassea di Pollo*

## CHICKEN MARSALA

### (my way)

SERVES 4

1 lb. chicken breast, thinly sliced
2 tablespoons flour
salt and pepper
6 tablespoons olive oil
3 large potatoes, sliced or cubed (about 6 to 8 slices
for each potato)
1 large onion, sliced
1 teaspoon oregano
1 teaspoon rosemary
1 cup marsala wine
1 medium jar marinated artichoke hearts, cut
in half
1 package shiitake mushrooms, cut into pieces

Wash chicken and pat dry. Add salt and pepper to flour and coat chicken. Heat 3 tablespoons of oil in a large skillet over medium heat. Sear chicken until golden on both sides to seal in juices. Remove from skillet.

In the same skillet, add 3 more tablespoons of oil and sauté the onions until golden brown. Add the mushrooms. Sauté for 2 minutes. Add the artichokes and sauté for another 2 minutes.

Raise the temperature to high. Add the marsala and cook for three minutes to let the wine evaporate. Set aside.

In a medium size non-stick baking dish, arrange the sliced potatoes and sprinkle with salt, pepper, oregano, and rosemary mixture. Place the chicken cutlets on top and cover it all with the marsala mixture.

Cover and bake at 400 degrees for about 30 minutes or until potatoes are tender. Take the cover off and bake for another 10 minutes on high. Serve with a nice fruity white wine.

## SPEZZATINO DI CARNE

SERVES 4

1 lb. sirloin tips
1 large onion, quartered
3 tablespoons olive oil
2–3 large potatoes, quartered
1 1/2 teaspoons salt (or to taste)
parsley
3/4 cup red wine
1 cup water
1 teaspoon pepper kernels
1/2 cup tomatoes, chopped (optional)

In a 4-quart non-stick saucepan, sauté onion in oil until tender. Add meat. Sprinkle with salt and sauté for about 10 minutes.

Add wine and cook for another 5 minutes on high.

Reduce the temperature and add potatoes, pepper kernels, parsley, and water. Stir. Cover and cook over low to medium heat until meat and potatoes are tender, stirring occasionally. Add additional water if needed, and salt according to taste.

*Spezzatino di Carne*

## NO FUSS FISH SOUP
**Brodo di Pesce**
SERVES 6

2 lbs. ocean perch or whiting
1/2 cup olive oil
3 garlic cloves, chopped
2 large tomatoes, peeled and chopped, or 1/2 cup canned
diced tomatoes
2 cups water
salt and pepper
3–4 sprigs fresh parsley
3 cups pastina (optional)

In a 5-quart pan, sauté garlic in oil until golden. Add tomatoes and salt and pepper to taste, and continue to sauté for about 5 minutes.

Add water and bring to a boil. Add fish and parsley. Semi-cover the pan and simmer for about 15 minutes over medium high heat. It can be eaten as a soup with some good Italian bread, or served alone by squeezing some lemon over it.

To make a full meal, cook 3 cups of pastina according to package directions. Once the pastina is almost cooked, discard some of the water from the pasta pan and replace it with the fish broth. Cook a few minutes more. Adjust the taste to your liking and serve.

*Brodo di Pesce, fish soup*

## SEASONED BREAD CRUMBS

1 lb. plain bread crumbs
1 cup grated Romano cheese
1 teaspoon pepper
1 teaspoon salt
1 tablespoon chopped parsley
1–2 garlic cloves, crushed or finely minced
(add an extra clove if you like the flavor of garlic)

Mix all ingredients together. If needed, adjust taste by adding salt and pepper and/or grated cheese.

Can be used to bread any type of fish, meat, or vegetable. Can also be used as stuffing.

When breading meats and vegetables, add 1 tablespoon of basil for added flavor. I prefer to use Panko, a Japanese style bread crumb. It is made from the inside of the bread, which is the old-fashioned Sicilian way.

For a Mediterranean bread crumb, replace parsley with 1 teaspoon oregano.

## SIMPLE ZABAGLIONE
**as a protein drink**

1 egg yolk
1 heaping tablespoon sugar
1 demitasse or more of hot espresso coffee
(or use 1/3 cup of your favorite coffee)

Beat egg yolk with sugar until pale and soft. Add the hot espresso, stir, and enjoy.

For a different flavor try it with warm milk, coffee liqueur, or Marsala. Delicious!

Our parents and grandparents served it to us every day for protein intake and energy.

## ZUPPA DI ZUCCHINE E PATATE

SERVES 4

1 large zucchini, cut into 1" cubes
1 large potato, cut into small cubes
1/2 cup fresh peeled tomato, chopped
3–4 tablespoons olive oil
salt and pepper to taste
1 small onion, diced
1 tablespoon parsley, chopped
3–4 cups water
2 slices Italian ham, cut into pieces
caciocavallo (optional)

In a 2-quart saucepan, heat oil and add chopped onion. Sauté until tender.

Add peeled tomatoes, parsley, and salt and pepper. Stir and continue to sauté for a minute, adding a little water to keep it from sticking to the pan. Sauté for about three minutes, then add the potatoes and sauté for a few minutes more.

Add zucchini and stir to mix all ingredients. Add the rest of the water and cook uncovered for about 20 minutes or until potatoes and zucchini are tender. Adjust flavor by adding salt and pepper if needed.

For more flavor, add some chopped caciocavallo and/or Italian ham. I like to add pasta to this soup. As such, halfway through the cooking of the potatoes and zucchini, I add 1–2 cups of hot water. Bring to a boil and then add 1 cup of ditalini or conchigliette and cook it right in the soup, adding more water if needed. Serve with grated Romano or Parmesan cheese.

## INSALATA CAMPAGNOLA

SERVES 6

4 large potatoes, peeled and boiled
1 lb. string beans, steamed
1 lb. fresh tomatoes (not ripe)
1 medium red onion, thinly sliced
1 teaspoon oregano
1/2 cup olive oil
1/4 cup white wine vinegar (or balsamic)
salt and pepper
olives and/or anchovies (optional)

Cut the potatoes, tomatoes, and beans into bite size pieces. Place all ingredients in a large serving bowl or in a salad dish. Salt and pepper to taste. Sprinkle the oregano and pour the oil and vinegar over it. Gently toss everything together and serve. For a variation of taste add your preferred type of olives or anchovies to salad. Delicious! Can be served hot or cold. A great picnic salad for summer outings.

*Insalata Campagnola, a fresh*
*string bean and potato salad*

## DOLCE DI MELE E BANANE

SERVES 6–8

4 eggs
1 cup sugar
2 1/2 tablespoons butter
1 lemon rind
1/4 cup cherry liqueur
2 1/2 cups flour
3 teaspoons baking powder
1 apple, cubed
1 apple, sliced
1 banana, cubed
1 banana, sliced
confectioners' sugar

Beat eggs with sugar and butter until pale and soft.

Add lemon rind, liqueur, flour, and baking powder. Mix well.

Add the cubed apples and bananas and mix thoroughly. Put the mixture into an 8" x 11" greased and floured pan. Shake to ensure that there are no bubbles.

Decorate with sliced apple and banana, dust with confectioners' sugar, and bake at 350 degrees for about one hour.

## STUFFED SUN DRIED TOMATOES

12 large sun dried tomatoes
1/2 cup seasoned bread crumbs
1–2 tablespoons olive oil
1 tablespoon tomato sauce
1 tablespoon chopped caciocavallo
cheese (optional)
olive oil

Soak the tomatoes for at least 6 hours to take the salt out. Drain and place each tomato on a paper towel to dry.

In a bowl, mix bread crumbs with oil and sauce, adding cheese if desired. Mixture should be moist. Add a little more oil if needed.

Take one half of a tomato and stuff it with about 1 teaspoon or more (depending on the size of the tomato) of the bread crumb. Cover with the other half of the tomato and press together to seal the stuffing. Continue to do so until you have stuffed all the tomatoes. Place them on a greased baking tray. Drizzle with oil and bake at 450 degrees for about 7–10 minutes on each side, or fry them in hot oil. Serve hot or cold as an appetizer. They taste even better the next day.

*Stuffed Sun Dried Tomatoes, served hot or cold, make a delicious appetizer.*

## ANELLETTI AL FORNO

SERVES 6–8

46 oz. tomato sauce (see page 14)
1 small package frozen petite peas
1 eggplant, cubed
1 lb. anelletti (small ring shaped pasta)
1 egg, beaten
8 oz. shredded mozzarella, divided
1 cup prosciutto cotto, cubed
1/2 cup grated Romano cheese
2–3 cups béchamel sauce or 1 cup ricotta cheese
fresh basil, chopped
olive oil
bread crumbs
salt and pepper to taste

Prepare tomato sauce and the peas halfway through the cooking. Sauce should be thin.

Sprinkle salt over eggplant and let sit for one hour.

Wash and dry eggplant. Heat enough oil in a skillet for frying and fry eggplant until golden brown. Drain on paper towels. Set aside.

Cook the pasta according to package directions, but make sure it is very "al dente" (not overcooked). Drain pasta and put it in a large bowl. Add 1/4 of the sauce, egg, 4 oz. of mozzarella, prosciutto, eggplant, 1/4 cup grated cheese, and one cup of béchamel sauce or 1 cup of ricotta cheese. Mix everything together.

Pour just enough tomato sauce to cover the bottom of a greased medium size baking dish. Form a layer with half of the pasta mixture, sauce, béchamel sauce, mozzarella, basil, a sprinkle of grated cheese, and some bread crumbs. Repeat process with another layer of pasta sauce and béchamel sauce. Finish by sprinkling more grated cheese and some extra bread crumbs, and adding a pinch of salt and freshly ground pepper. Drizzle with a little olive oil.

Cover and bake at 400 degrees for 20 minutes. Uncover and bake for another 10 minutes or until a little golden crust forms. Cool 10 minutes before serving. Pour any leftover sauce over dish.

## BASIC BÉCHAMEL SAUCE

2 tablespoons butter
2 tablespoons all-purpose flour
1 cup warm milk
1/2 teaspoon salt
pinch of white pepper
freshly ground nutmeg (optional)

Melt butter in a saucepan over medium heat. Add flour and stir until mixture is well blended. Gradually stir in warm milk. Cook over medium heat, stirring constantly, until sauce begins to boil and thickens. Add a pinch of nutmeg. Stir and use immediately.

*Anelletti al Forno, a hearty baked pasta dish.*

## TORTA MOKA

SERVES 4

2 eggs
1/2 cup sugar
2 tablespoons + 1/4 teaspoon melted butter, cooled
1 demitasse very strong espresso coffee
1 teaspoon vanilla
3/4 cup flour
3 teaspoons baking powder

In a bowl, beat eggs and sugar until soft.

Add the butter, coffee, vanilla, flour, and baking powder.

Work the mixture for about ten minutes and pour into a greased and floured cake pan.

Bake at 375 degrees for 1/2 hour or until done. Cool and decorate to your liking or eat just as it is.


## CUCCIDDATA (Old fashioned recipe)

MAKES 5 DOZEN

2 lbs. + 3 oz. flour
1 cup + 2 tablespoons sugar
1 cup + 2 tablespoons shortening
5 teaspoons ammonium bicarbonate
2 1/2 teaspoons baking powder
1 teaspoon vanilla
1 large egg, lightly beaten
1 1/4 cups lukewarm milk

Icing: 1 lb. confectioners' sugar and 3–4 tablespoons milk

In a large bowl, combine dry ingredients. Add shortening. Mixture should resemble a coarse meal. Make a well.

In a separate bowl, beat together egg, milk, and vanilla. Add the egg mixture to the dry ingredients.

Mix thoroughly to make a soft cookie dough. Add more milk if needed.

This is a basic cookie dough for making plain cookies or any type of filled cookies.

Bake at 400 for 10 minutes or until golden.

Icing: Combine confectioners' sugar and 3–4 tablespoons of milk. Add more liquid if necessary. Spread with your fingers to cover the cookies. Sprinkle with colored pralines if desired.


## FIG FILLING

1 lb. fig preserves
1/4 cup dates, chopped
1/4 cup mini chocolate chips
1/4 cup almonds, chopped
1/4 cup raisins, chopped
1/4 cup pine nuts, chopped
1 orange rind, grated
1 tablespoon cinnamon
1/4 cup orange citron

In a bowl, combine above ingredients using your hands. Mix well. To fill cookies, take a handful of dough and roll it out to a round circle, about 1/4" thick. Place 1 teaspoon of filling in the center. Close the dough by wrapping it into the center, making sure nothing is exposed. Turn dough upside down and scallop the edges to decorate.

This filling can be stored in the refrigerator for up to one year.

*Cucciddata, a white cookie
with sweet fig filling*

The world-famous marble quarries at Carrara, which have drawn sculptors from Michelangelo to Henry Moore, figure prominently in the life of Margherita Bancarotta Pelliccia as do the fishing waters surrounding northern Tuscany and Cape Ann.

Margherita grew up in the Tuscan seaside resort of Viareggio known for its Lenten Carnival, beaches, palm-lined esplanade, grand hotels, and Art Nouveau buildings. Her father, a commercial fisherman, moved the family to this port on the Tyrrhenian Sea when she was a toddler because the fishing here was so much better than off their native Terrasini, Sicily.

Margherita attended school in Viareggio, spending her formative years enjoying the cuisine of the region, whose specialties she prepares for her family in Gloucester today.

In Viareggio, a culinary favorite consists of *cecina*, a light mouthwatering chickpea pancake, wrapped in foccacia. Often people will eat this as a late afternoon *merenda* or snack, since they often don't eat dinner till 8:30 or 9 p.m., says Margherita. You can make *foccacia* and *cecina* at home, as she does, and, when in Viareggio, you can enjoy this combination or *cecina* alone, seasoned with salt and pepper, at a pizzeria.

In Gloucester Margherita, her husband, Franco, and other family members frequently eat a breakfast consisting of coffee and foccacia with cold cuts or with *cecina*, called *farinata* in Franco's hometown of Carrara.

Mention Carrara, where Franco spent the first decade of his working life quarrying the celebrated white marble, and both he and Margherita will wax nostalgic. Speaking about the quarries in the Apuan

Alps, which have been excavated since Roman times, he says: "Once you see, you never forget. They are something you cannot believe, very beautiful."

Margherita elaborates: "In Carrara, the whole mountain is white. You look up and it looks like snow. But it's not, it's white marble. And then to walk in the mountains and touch the cut stone!"

At home in Gloucester, Margherita shows a visitor old black and white photographs displaying how blocks of marble were once ferried down the Apuan mountains on wooden rollers and then carried to the port by oxen-drawn wagons. For a time, a railway transported the quarried stone, and today trucks traverse the mountain roads, removing some 1.5 million tons a year of quarried Apuan marble.

Besides photos and memories, the Pelliccias possess several small round pieces of the fine white Carrara marble, momentos inlaid into their stone fireplace, reminding them of a place they will always love.

Margherita and Franco met and fell in love in Viareggio. They married in 1973 and came to Gloucester soon after. Here on Cape Ann Franco worked briefly at Gorton's (as did Margherita). Then, after they were laid off, he followed her brother and father into commercial fishing.

For many years Franco worked as the cook and engineer on the fishing vessel *Paul and Dominic*, making ten to 12 day trips to Georges Bank to fish for groundfish. Several years ago, when Captain Tom Brancaleone sold that boat and retired, Franco took a site on the dragger *Padre Pio*, where he still works today. Because of severe cuts in allowable fishing days, it has become increasingly difficult not

*Franco Pelliccia with a large cod onboard the* Pardre Pio.

Photo courtesy of Jeff Rotman Photography

only to make a living fishing, but to plan for retirement, says Margherita. This is one reason she and Franco insisted that their children go to college rather than fish.

Their daughter, 29, works as a preschool teacher in Gloucester, and their son, 25, as a personal trainer at the Fitness Zone here. To help put the two through college, Margherita worked at Oakwood Nursing Home. Today, besides maintaining the household, she takes care of her ailing mother.

The Pelliccias are in good company here on Cape Ann. The first Italians to settle on this rocky peninsula also arrived from the North with stone cutting expertise. A century ago they put these skills to work in the now abandoned granite quarries in Lanesville and Rockport.

## FOCACCIA

SERVES 6

1 lb. flour
1 package yeast or 1 yeast cake
3 tablespoons olive oil
1/2 tablespoon salt
1 cup warm water
salt and pepper

In a large bowl, mix flour with yeast and salt. Make a well in the middle and add the warm water.

Knead the dough for about 10 minutes or until smooth and elastic. Add more water or flour if necessary. Brush the top of the dough with a little oil, then cover with a cotton towel and a small blanket. Let it rise about one hour or until it doubles in volume.

Divide the dough in half and knead again for 5 minutes. Use a rolling pin or your hands to stretch the dough. Transfer onto a greased cookie sheet. Sprinkle with a little olive oil and spread it throughout the dough. Sprinkle with salt and pepper. Let dough rest for about 5 minutes. This will allow it to become less elastic and easier to spread.

With your fingertips, make prints throughout the dough. Let it rise for another 1/2 hour, uncovered and in a warm place. Bake at 400 degrees for about 1/2 hour or until golden brown.

## CECINA

2 cups chickpea flour
4 cups lukewarm water
2 tablespoons olive oil
1 teaspoon salt
1 teaspoon pepper

In a medium bowl, mix the chickpea flour and salt and pepper.

Using a whisk, slowly add water to the mixture, beating it to avoid lumps.

Pour the mixture into an oil-greased 15" x 10" x 1" jellyroll pan. Bake at 400 degrees for about 20 minutes. Cut into squares and serve between hot focaccia.

*Eastern Point Lighthouse*
Photo courtesy of Sharon's Studio of Gloucester

"It's a good thing I like fish because it's fed me most of my life," says 26-year-old Rosandra Brancaleone. "At home we ate fish four nights a week—cod, haddock, lobster, shrimp, and scallops. My favorites are scallops and grey sole. My father filleted the sole on the boat and brought it home, and we breaded it and baked it with olive oil."

When Rosandra was growing up, her father, Gaetano (Tom) Brancaleone, a commercial fisherman, was at sea for ten days at a time. He has since retired. Her mother, Mary, always self-reliant, encouraged the same in Rosandra. "At two-and-a-half I was loading dishes into the dishwasher and at four, I was making my own scrambled eggs and helping my Mom to bread the fish."

A bright and energetic young woman who works as a software trainer, Rosandra was "primarily raised by my mother because my dad was always fishing. I remember how excited I was when he returned from a fishing trip. My mother and I would go down to the wharf to meet him. I would jump out of the car and run down to the boat, try to jump on the boat and run to find my father. He was usually in the engine room, checking things out. He would pick me up and swing me around. Even though he smelled, from not showering for 10 days, I didn't care. I was just excited to see him."

"My grandmother always took pride in her son, my father. When he came home, we'd have a celebration, a big lunch with the entire family. It was a relief to have everyone home; it was just like, 'he came home; he made it. Nothing happened' because you hear of so many tragedies out there and you know it really hits home when you know the person who gets lost."

"I often wished my Dad was there for special events, mainly my birthdays. He'd always call on my birthday, always call from out at sea or have balloons sent to me, or flowers. He always remembered, but he was never physically there." Even though her father was away much of the time, Rosandra says she feels blessed by her parents' "unconditional love. There was never a moment where they didn't care what I did."

"My parents always took me places. I know some people who never went to Disney World till they were married. I went there a lot when I was little. I loved to travel; my suitcase was always packed. I was never deprived of anything. I hope my own kids get as much."

Rosandra attended Gloucester public schools, ran track, and played basketball and softball. "Most of the friends I hung out with were Italian. My cousin was my best friend. She was three days younger than me. I also had a couple of American friends and some Portuguese. It didn't make any difference. We'd play house, we'd play kick the can, we'd play hide n' seek. Or we'd pretend we were going on an adventure and make a trail map and follow it."

"The happiest times in my childhood were always the holidays when the entire family was together. I'm very close to my second, third, and fourth cousins on my dad's side. We keep in contact; we write and visit each other in California, Canada, Michigan—all over. The saddest moment was the suicide of my cousin." When Rosandra was in college and facing difficult challenges, she remembers, "I'd pray to God to send me an angel and my cousin would appear to me in a dream, reassuring me that things will be okay."

Rosandra never considered a fishing career. "My father would never let me. He considered it too dangerous." He likewise discouraged her brothers from fishing "because he knew it was a hard life." However, they pitched in summers helping him to paint and repair the boat, while also making a few fishing trips. "The summer I was in the seventh grade, I remember talking over the marine radio. I told Nico [Domenic] how I was winning my softball games and I remember him telling me how he was throwing up over the side of the boat!"

Tom and Mary Brancaleone encouraged all three children to go to college. Paul, now 36, studied history and business at Boston University and owns his own business; Domenic, 33, majored in engineering at Purdue University and works as Computer Networker. Rosandra studied Information Systems, first at the University of South Florida and later at Northeastern University in Boston, from which she earned a bachelor of science degree.

In Florida, far from home and surrounded by classmates from many different countries, Rosandra developed a new appreciation for her own Sicilian-American heritage. For two years she served as president of the Italian Club, arranging for many cross cultural events with students from all over the world. A third-generation Italian-American, she wants to enrich her understanding of her own cultural heritage and also to encourage others to do the same.

Before taking a job at a software company in San Diego, California, Rosandra worked as the receptionist at the Gloucester Fishermen and Family Assistance Center, which helps hard-pressed fishermen and their families to find other work. For nearly a decade she has volunteered with the Gloucester Fishermen's Wives Association. "My mother didn't encourage me to get involved. It's something I wanted to do."

During her senior year in high school and summers during college, Rosandra traveled with the Wives to demonstrate fish cookery at supermarkets, seafood festivals, and fairs. She attended meetings, and worked behind the scenes on the Fishermen's Wives Memorial. "It was awesome being around during the creation and erection of the statue." Becoming increasingly committed to the work of the GFWA, Rosandra joined its board and that of the Memorial's.

"I come from a long line of fishermen. The fishing industry has affected my family in so many ways. The GFWA helps to keep the fishing culture going. And the Wives have given me something to remember for the rest of my life—the three virtues inscribed in stone on the Boulevard—faith, diligence, and fortitude."

## CHICKEN WRAPPED IN PROSCUITTO
SERVES 4

4 pieces chicken breast
8 1" balls fresh mozzarella cheese, diced
1/2 cup sun dried tomatoes in oil, diced
fresh basil leaves, diced
1 cup chicken broth
1 cup red wine
8 slices proscuitto

In a skillet, combine wine and chicken broth. Bring to a boil.

In the meantime, in a bowl, combine cheese, tomatoes, and basil. Set aside.

Slice the chicken breast down the side and stuff with cheese mixture. Wrap the chicken with the prosciutto and tie it with a string.

Place chicken in the skillet and simmer for 15–20 minutes or until it is done, turning once.

Remove chicken from skillet and place on a platter. Pour wine mixture over the chicken and serve.

"Tlove food, and I love to cook. But I have to have a recipe in front of me. I cannot do things out of my head. Even if I'm cooking a dish I made up, I still need to consult the list of ingredients," says Connie Condon, the longtime marketing director of *A Taste of Gloucester: A Fisherman's Wife Cooks*, the Gloucester Fishermen's Wives Association's cookbook. The popular spiral bound cookbook, written in cooperation with the Cape Ann League of Women Voters, is now in its eighth printing, having sold 200,000 copies around the world.

A registered nurse by profession, Connie taught herself how to cook by reading cookbooks and trying out new recipes. Along the way she became a cookbook collector. At one time she owned 1,400 volumes, all in English, from a half-dozen countries and all over the United States. Recently, she's been divesting herself of some of the books by donating them to charitable organizations.

Connie is especially passionate about Italian and Asian cuisine. Her Fish Balls recipe came out of years of Asian cookery. "I cooked my first Asian dish, Chinese Sweet and Sour Pork, when my children were one-and-a-half, two-and-a-half, and three-and-a-half years old. I was following a recipe from a little booklet I got from Le Choy. I still have the book. I cut the pork into small cubes, and, while I was making the sauce, our cat, who was pregnant, decided to have her kittens in a box, right in the middle of the kitchen floor! The kids brought in those little Mexican straw chairs and sat and watched the whole procedure while I stirred the sauce. The dish came out perfect!"

When Connie and her husband, Bob, and their children moved to Gloucester, she says, "I knew noth-ing about cooking fish. Lena [Novello] taught me everything I know today about cooking seafood. She taught me how to fry calamari, the right temperature at which to steam lobsters and steamers, how to cook haddock, pollock, whiting. I'd never done any of this before."

Connie has been a mainstay of the GFWA for nearly 30 years. Lena Novello, a GFWA founder and the matriarch of the Gloucester fishing community, reeled her in. She invited Connie and her husband, Bob, to a fundraising breakfast at Cameron's Restau-rant during the campaign to pass the US's 200-mile limit law. Lena and the other Fisher-men's Wives had seen their husband's catches decimated by a fleet of for-eign factory trawlers working off the New England coast, some within clear view of Gloucester. The Wives were raising money to travel to Washington with a dory bearing hundreds of signatures to demon-strate support for the 200-mile limit. *The Gloucester Daily Times* published a page one photograph of Bob and others signing the dory.

The Condons did not go to Washington, but they became active locally. Bob was the first man to join the GFWA. He and Connie pitched in at GFWA bake sales, cooking demonstrations, everything. From this a strong friendship flowered. "Lena is my best friend," says Connie. "She is like a mother and sister to me. She not only embraced me, she embraced my husband and children, as well."

"Lena became the grandmother my kids never had," adds Bob. "They adopted her and she and her children adopted us, as family."

When the Wives went on the road with their cook-book, Connie accompanied them. She learned to cook some of the recipes and helped pitch in preparing and serving fish. Over the years she and other GFWA members have traveled to supermarkets, schools, seafood festivals, and even the Smithsonian Museum to demonstrate some of the many ways to cook fish. At the Smithsonian, the Wives conducted a symposium "What's the Catch?" showing people how to prepare herring burgers. The Wives brought "pounds and pounds of fish." The herring burgers "were so popular we ran out of them," remembers Connie.

In October 2000 Connie attended the World Fisheries Forum in Loctudy, Brittany, France, as an East Coast observer. "Seeing and hearing fishing representatives from 26 countries was a great experience, one I will always remember," she says. "It made me realize that the problems fishermen face are universal." Several years earlier, at a meeting of Non-Governmental Organizations at the United Nations, Connie delivered a heartfelt plea calling for an end to destructive factory trawling worldwide.

While Connie Condon did not grow up or marry into a fishing family, her daughter, Mary Clare, a dental hygienist, did, making Connie the mother-in-law of a commercial lobsterman. She and Bob also have a son, Robert Jr., a lawyer. Their other son, Michael, died of cancer when he was 16.

Michael loved to fish, Connie remembers. His last summer "he spent many hours down on the wharf fishing. He also helped out on the Yankee Fleet. He used to bring the fish home and make a terrible mess in the kitchen. There'd be flour from one end of the room to the other. He'd fry up the fish and eat them! Had Michael lived he would have gone fishing with Lena's husband, Joe. I know Michael would have been a fisherman."

The Fishermen's Wives Memorial is especially important to Connie, who, like other GFWA activists, helped fundraise for it. ("Lena and I went to visit the head of Gorton's; they donated $20,000 for two large granite benches.")

"From its inception," says Connie, "I thought of the Memorial as a statue that honors not just fisher-

*The Gloucester Fishermen's Wives Memorial, overlooking Gloucester Harbor, is a tribute to the wives of fishermen and mariners everywhere, and also honors women worldwide for their selfless contributions to their families and communities.*
Photo by Peter Prybot

men's wives, but all women because women are the ones who take care of the children and keep the family together while their husbands are away fighting wars, flying for the airlines, and working other jobs that keep them away from home, including, of course, fishing. It's the women who hold the community together."

## GREAT FISHBALLS

MAKES 35-40 FISHBALLS

Sauce:
10 oz. sweet and sour sauce
1/4 cup chicken broth
2 tablespoons soy sauce
1/2 teaspoon garlic powder

Fishballs:
1 1/2 lbs. white fish such as haddock, pollock, catfish, or cod
1 8-oz. can water chestnuts, drained and chopped
2 eggs
1/3 cup bread crumbs
2 tablespoons soy sauce
2 tablespoons scallions, chopped
1/2 teaspoon each garlic powder and ground ginger

Sauce:
In a large saucepan, combine sauce ingredients. Cook, stirring constantly until mixture is thick and bubbly. Remove from heat and set aside.

Fishballs:
In a large bowl, combine fishball ingredients and form into 1" balls. Place on a baking sheet. Bake at 425 degrees for 15 minutes. Add to sauce. Cook for 10–15 minutes.

## SALSA VERDE

**(green sauce)**

2 eggs, hardboiled
1 loaf Italian bread
6 tablespoons white wine vinegar
3 oz. Italian parsley
1 garlic clove
6 salted anchovy fillets in oil
1 teaspoon capers
1 1/3 cups olive oil
salt and pepper to taste

Shell eggs and discard the whites. Set yolk aside.

Remove the inside of the Italian bread and place 2 oz. of it into a bowl. Add the vinegar.

Remove the bread from the vinegar by squeezing out the vinegar with your hands.

In a mixer or food processor, place parsley, garlic, egg yolks, anchovies, bread, capers, and oil. Add salt and pepper to taste. Mix until sauce is soft and homogenous.

This sauce is excellent with boiled meat, grilled fish such as tuna and mackerel, boiled fish, hardboiled eggs, and dropped eggs.

## OLANDESE SAUCE

2 tablespoons white wine vinegar
3 tablespoons white wine
1 tablespoon water
3 egg yolks, beaten
10 tablespoons butter, cut into small pieces
salt and pepper to taste

In a small saucepan, bring vinegar and wine to a boil. Reduce to one tablespoon.

Using a double boiler, place enough water in the lower pan to heat the top pan. Pour wine mixture in top pan. Add 1 tablespoon of water, eggs yolks, and a small piece of butter. Beat the ingredients together until whipped. Add the rest of the butter one piece at a time, stirring constantly.

Remove from the heat. Salt and pepper to taste.

This sauce is best over broiled fish, steamed vegetables, and boiled potatoes.

## BLUEBERRY BREAD

2 eggs, beaten
1 cup sour milk
1/2 cup brown sugar
1/3 cup olive oil
1 cup rolled oats
2 cups flour, sifted
1 teaspoon baking powder
1 teaspoon baking soda
1 teaspoon salt
1/2 teaspoon cinnamon
1 cup nuts, chopped
1 1/2 cups blueberries, frozen or fresh
1/2 cup raisins

In a large bowl, combine eggs, milk, brown sugar, olive oil, and rolled oats.

In a separate bowl, combine flour, baking powder, baking soda, salt, and cinnamon. Combine with egg mixture until blended. Gently fold in nuts, blueberries, and raisins.

Pour batter into a 9" x 5" x 3" loaf pan and bake at 350 degrees for one hour. Cool for a few minutes before removing from pan and placing on a cooling rack.

*P*riscilla Decker-Evans, 83, enjoyed a relatively privileged childhood as the daughter of a successful Gloucester fishing captain. Her father, Andrew Decker, commanded vessels including the schooner *Imperator* used in the classic 1937 film, "Captain's Courageous."

"I never felt deprived," says Priscilla, who was born in Gloucester and grew up there during the Depression. When money was tight, "my mother would say, 'we can't do it this week, we'll do it when Daddy comes in.'"

Gloucester grocer Hank Souza proved a godsend to the Deckers and other fishing families because he allowed his customers to pay on account. "My mother would buy the groceries for the boat as well our family. She would pay the bill when my father got home."

"My mother used to listen to WHDH radio. At 10 am they would announce the names of the boats that had come into Boston that day and what they had caught. They would also report the prices; my mother would know even before my father came home whether it had been a good trip." If so, "we would get dressed up and go to the Chinese restaurant, which was right across the street from Broad's shoe store on the second floor."

Priscilla's mother, the former Annie Lori Sheehan of Gloucester, ran the household like a tight ship. For the sake of cleanliness, she required that all five children remove their shoes in the house. She would not allow Priscilla or her siblings to help out in the kitchen, and she maintained a strict protocol when hanging the wash on the outside line: "the good sheets went on the outside; therefore the next-door neighbor didn't see the other clothes."

As Priscilla remembers it, "my mother was the first woman in Gloucester to own a washing machine, the ugliest thing you ever did see. My father went by the Electric Light Company on Main Street and bought a Maytag. I can never remember my mother without a washing machine."

Even so, Andrew Decker "never brought dirty clothes home from a fishing trip. He would bring them to one of the boarding houses on Duncan and Rogers Streets, where women took in washing. Then he would pick them up before the next trip."

Young Priscilla "often went to the movies because there was no TV; it cost ten cents for children under 12, and, of course we never aged over 12!" She played with dolls and doll carriages, enjoyed checkers, and rode a bicycle. Her family owned "a radio with a battery. Every Saturday a man would come to charge it or replace the old battery with a new one."

As she grew older, Priscilla sometimes took the train into Boston to meet her father at the Fish Pier. "I had all the warnings as to whom to talk to and whom not to talk to." While she never fished with her father (that would have been unheard of for a girl of her era) she went aboard the boat "to watch the famous schooners race—the *Blue Nose* and *Gertrude L. Thibault.*"

Her father, a graduate of the Boston School of Navigation (now Massachusetts Maritime Academy), gave up command of merchant ships and switched to fishing partly because the trips were shorter. As a merchant seaman, he had been at sea for three months at a time. By contrast, his fishing trips lasted only two to three weeks. Still this could be a long stretch for a young child. During one homecoming, Priscilla's brother, Andrew, then five, did not recognize their father. The boy ran into the house, shouting, "mommy, that man is coming!"

During World War II, Andrew Decker served as an observer for the US Coast Guard. "If he spotted anything unusual, he would report it. We had blackouts every night and pulled the shades right to the bottom," remembers Priscilla.

A native of Shelburne, Nova Scotia, her father had been raised as a Baptist; her mother was Catholic. Priscilla and her siblings were raised in their mother's faith.

The Deckers moved to Rockport in 1938, when Priscilla was 17. Soon after she spotted a "help wanted" sign in a restaurant window. "I did what no one would do today: I ran home to get my mother to come with me to apply. I earned $3.50 a week. I was able to buy my own clothes and I had plenty of spending money."

After graduating from Rockport High School, Priscilla went to business school.

She married Robert Evans, who worked in the post office in Gloucester. They have a daughter, Roberta Evans, a nurse; two granddaughters; two great grandsons, and two great granddaughters.

*Captain Andrew Decker in 1908 at age 22.*

## CODFISH CASSEROLE

SERVES 6

2 1/2 cups fresh codfish, cooked and flaked
4 tablespoons butter
2 tablespoons flour
1 teaspoon salt
1/4 teaspoon pepper
2 cups heated milk
1 cup grated Parmesan cheese
1/4 cup capers
fresh parsley, chopped
ground cayenne pepper

Melt butter in a medium saucepan. Add flour and salt and pepper. Stir to paste. Add milk and bring to a boil, stirring constantly. Continue boiling for 2 minutes. Remove from heat.

Grease a 2-quart casserole dish and pour a small amount of the sauce into the dish. Add a layer of codfish and sprinkle with cheese, capers, and sauce. Repeat layers until all ingredients are used. Top casserole with a sprinkling of cheese and capers.

Bake at 350 for 30 minutes or until nicely browned. Sprinkle with parsley and ground cayenne pepper.

As an award-winning landscape designer and a fisherman's daughter, Ann Gilardi Johnson seemed the ideal choice to landscape the Fishermen's Wives Memorial, unveiled in August 2001. Prior to this she had helped create parks, playgrounds, and open spaces from Quangdong Province, China, to Boston's Chinatown, but she had never worked in her hometown. Memorial Plaza, Ann's first Gloucester design, which occupies a 2,635-square foot site on Stacey Boulevard, received a 2002 merit award from the Boston Society of Landscape Architects.

"With all that exposure to wind and sea and noise and traffic" (the Fishermen's Wives monument stands at the junction of Routes 133 and 127 overlooking Gloucester Harbor) "this was not an easy site," says Ann. Aggravating matters were the inherent limits of the long, narrow waterfront lot. Ann faced considerable challenges creating a setting for visitors to appreciate Morgan Faulds Pike's powerful eight-foot tall bronze statue and the surrounding sea and sky.

"When I received the plot plan I was a little horrified," confides Ann, who holds a graduate certificate in landscape design from Radcliffe Seminars/Radcliffe College. "The boulder was already there. Photos of the monument were all over town. The Wives had commissioned large and small benches and were requesting donations for various sizes of paving stones. It seemed that they may have been hiring me to put in shrubs and flowers."

"'Good heavens,' I thought. 'This monument deserves so much more!'" After carefully studying the site and conferring with the sculptor, Ann made two decisions: to go with an oval-shaped concept, and "since the granite boulder was already there, to use native stone. From that the design evolved."

Since the Wives had committed to benches, "it made sense to design seat walls. I listened carefully to the Wives. They wanted to provide a certain amount of serenity to contemplate the beauty of the ocean and of the statue. They wanted the place to feel quiet even if it could not be quiet. I thought that the seat walls with their backs would absorb some of the noise, and they do."

The next challenge involved incorporating the many small and large paving stones with people's inscriptions. "We had to invent a paving pattern," says Ann. To organize the paving stones, she created a ring of granite around the irregularly-shaped boulder. She chose beach stones to fill the inside of the ring, and the Wives inscribed their dedication along the perimeter: "The wives, mothers, daughters, and sisters of Gloucester fishermen honor the wives and families of fishermen and mariners everywhere for their faith, diligence, and fortitude."

Donald Johnson, the owner of a former Rockport quarry, donated much of the native granite used to build the four seat walls that form an oval-shaped enclosure around the Wives' statue. Gloucester's Department of Public Works provided the rest. The cut paving stones and the smaller granite benches along the two pathways come from a still operative quarry in Chelmsford.

Sixty rose bushes grace the Fishermen's Wives Memorial. Ann selected Betty Prior, a hardy old-fashioned single blossom rose, whose explosion of hot pink flowers extends from late spring until at least the first frost. During Thanksgiving 2004 visitors were still enjoying the blooms. The brutally cold winter

*Site of the Gloucester Fishermen's Wives Memorial*
Photo courtesy of David Stotzer, Cape Ann Photography

before, the roses died; last spring the plants had to be replaced. Besides the roses, Ann blankets the site with colorful annuals. Last year she selected purple petunias and landscape contractor Kate Wiggin and her all-female crew, who tend the flowers, put in 800 of these plants; another year, Ann picked pink annuals, and the first year, ocean blue ones.

"I'm a firm believer in lots of color," says Ann, "but there shouldn't be so much that it's distracting. After all, the focal point is the sculpture. The landscaping needs to take a back seat to that."

For the landscape artist, "any design becomes a collaboration. If the designer does not listen to the artist and the constituency, it's not a good design."

Ann was born in Cambridge and grew up in Gloucester. Her father and older brother fished here in New England as had her grandfathers in Sciacca, Sicily. Ann's parents, Angelina and Michael Gilardi, valued education but were not prepared for her decision to go to college. After graduating from St. Ann's High School, Ann attended Merrimack College in North Andover, graduating with a bachelor of science degree in medical technology. For 15 years she worked in microbiology laboratories.

In 1983, unhappy in lab work, Ann decided to return to school. Her husband, Martin Johnson, had already made some career changes of his own. At the time their son, Kevin, was 13. Ann completed the Radcliffe program in 1986, immediately landing a job with the Boston Redevelopment Authority. During the following seven years, she worked closely with architects, planners, and community groups to realize a wide range of Boston projects, including James Hayes Park on the South End, which received three awards. The next five years she contracted work with the city of Worcester.

Ann has put her career on hold, for now, anyway, to care for her ailing mother. As the oldest daughter in a family with seven children, Ann now marvels at what she once took for granted—the life of a fisherman's wife. "My mother had to be practical; with good and bad years, she had to know how to make do and stretch the budget. She had to double everything and multitask. I remember her painting the front porch in-between cooking and doing the laundry and taking care of all of us. The life of a fisherman's wife is very hard and unique. It definitely builds character! That's why the Wives are so incredible!"

## LENTIL SOUP

SERVES 4

1 cup lentils
4 cups water
1/2 cup carrots, chopped
1/2 cup onions, chopped
1/2 cup celery, chopped
1/3 cup olive oil
salt and pepper to taste
1 cup ditalini pasta (optional)

Wash lentils and place in a pot with the water. Add carrots, onions, celery, and oil.

Bring to a boil without covering the pot. Salt and pepper to taste. Simmer until the lentils are soft. To cook pasta, add 1–2 cups hot water. Add pasta and cook until al dente.

## CAULIFLOWER SOUP

SERVES 4–6

1 cauliflower head
1 1/2 cups water
1/3 cup olive oil
4 garlic cloves, chopped
salt and pepper
1 pkg ditalini pasta (optional)
1/3 cup Romano cheese, small cubes

Remove cauliflower flowerets and cut into small pieces.

In a saucepan, combine the first 4 ingredients. Cover with water and bring to a boil, and then simmer until flowerets are soft.

Add 3 cups of hot water and ditalini. Cook until al dente. Add cheese and serve.

## EGGPLANT PARMESAN

SERVES 6–8

3 eggplants, washed and sliced into 1/4" rounds
flour for dredging
2 eggs, beaten
2 cups seasoned bread crumbs
olive oil for frying
28-oz. tomato sauce (see page 14)
3 cups mozzarella cheese
1/2 cup Romano or Parmesan cheese, grated

Coat eggplant with flour and then dip in egg. Dredge in bread crumbs until coated. Press crumbs into eggplant.

Heat a skillet with olive oil until the oil is very hot but not smoking.

Fry eggplant slices until golden brown, turning them once. Drain on paper towels.

In a baking pan, layer eggplant, mozzarella cheese, and tomato sauce. Sprinkle the top of each layer with grated cheese.

Sprinkle top with a little olive oil. Cover with foil and bake at 350 degrees for 30 minutes. Uncover and cook until cheese is golden.

## STUFFED ARTICHOKES

6 fresh artichokes
1 lemon, cut in half
2 cups seasoned bread crumbs (see page 93)
1/2 cup olive oil

Remove the first two layers of leaves from the artichokes. Using a serrated knife, cut the top half of each artichoke. Gently spread open the leaves of the artichoke without breaking them. Wash the artichokes and remove the center cavity. Turn them upside-down and drain. Rub lemon juice on the artichokes to prevent browning. Set aside.

Mix the bread crumbs with the oil until the crumbs are moist. Pack each cavity with the mixture.

Place artichokes in a deep skillet. Add enough water to cover 1/2 of the artichokes. Cover and steam the artichokes for 30 minutes or until tender.

## STUFFED PEPPERS

3/4 seasoned cup bread crumbs (see page 93)
1 lb. ground beef
2 eggs, beaten
6 green peppers
28 oz. tomato sauce (see page 14)
oil for frying

In a bowl, combine ground beef, bread crumbs, and eggs. Mix well.

Wash peppers and cut them in half. Remove seeds.

Fill each pepper with the meat mixture.

Heat a skillet with oil. Turn the peppers so the meat side is down and fry in olive oil until the meat is sealed in the pepper. Remove.

Place peppers in a greased baking dish, with the stuffing facing up. Cover the peppers with sauce and then with aluminum foil. Bake at 350 degrees for 25 minutes or until done. Uncover and cook for 10 more minutes.

## POTATOES, PEPPERS, AND EGGS
SERVES 4

2 lbs. potatoes, peeled and cubed
2 green peppers, seeded and sliced lengthwise
1/3 cup olive oil
1/2 lb. pre-cooked meat, optional (sausage or salami)
3 eggs, beaten
salt and pepper to taste

Boil potatoes in salted water in a large skillet until barely tender. Drain and cool slightly.

Heat oil in a skillet and sauté potatoes and peppers. Stir gently to prevent sticking. Add meat and continue cooking for about 10 minutes. Add eggs and salt and pepper to taste. Cover and cook until done.

## FISH CAKES
SERVES 4–6

1 cup bread crumbs (see page 93)
2 lbs. haddock or cod
2 eggs
vegetable oil for frying

Place fish in a pot and add enough water to cover the fish. Poach fish until it flakes. Drain. Flake fish and place in a bowl.

Add bread crumbs and eggs. Mix until moist. Form mixture into oval cakes.

In a deep skillet, heat enough oil for frying. A deep fryer is best.

Fry the cakes until golden brown. Do not turn them too soon, as they will fall apart.

Serve with salad and Italian bread.

## CARROT SOUFFLÉ
SERVES 6–8

2 cups carrots, peeled, cooked, and mashed (easy to cook in microwave)
1/4 cup butter, melted
1/2 cup white sugar
3 eggs
1/2 teaspoon cinnamon
1 tablespoon flour
1 teaspoon baking powder
1 cup whole milk or light cream

In a bowl, mix together carrots, butter, and sugar.

In a separate bowl, beat together eggs and cinnamon. Add to carrot mixture.

Add flour, baking powder and milk. Beat well.

Pour into a large casserole dish. Do not cover.

Bake immediately at 350 degrees for 45 minutes or until set.

## CANNOLI FILLING
MAKES 8

Purchase the shells, either large or small, as they are difficult to make. An Italian bakery or a specialty store will usually stock them. Below are two ways of making ricotta filling.

Filling 1:
2 cups ricotta (use whole milk ricotta)
1/2 cup confectioners' sugar
1/4 teaspoon vanilla
3 tablespoons chopped semi sweet chocolate
1/2 teaspoon cinnamon

Filling 2:
1 pound ricotta
1 tablespoon orange peel, grated
4 tablespoons granulated white sugar
1 teaspoon cinnamon

Mix ingredients well. Fill the shells with a small spoon or a pastry flute. Sprinkle the shells lightly with confectioners' sugar and drip the ends in crushed pistachio nuts. Serve immediately as the shells will become soggy.

## HERMITS
MAKES 4 DOZEN

3/4 cup shortening
1 cup brown sugar (packed)
1 egg
1/3 cup molasses
2 1/4 cups flour
2 teaspoons baking soda
1/2 teaspoon cloves
1 teaspoon cinnamon
1 teaspoon ginger
1 teaspoon allspice
1 cup chopped nuts
1 cup currants

In a bowl, cream together shortening, sugar, egg, and molasses.

In a separate bowl, combine flour, baking soda, cloves, cinnamon, ginger, and allspice.

Combine egg and flour mixture. Add nuts and currants. Work with hands until dough is smooth. Dough should be firm but not dry. Add water if necessary.

Shape dough into long loaves, about 2" wide by 1 1/2" high.

Bake at 375 degrees. Watch the loaves carefully, as they will puff and then set. Remove from oven before they set firmly. Cut into 1-2" slices.

## APPLE PIE

Crust:
MAKES 4 CRUSTS (two pies, top and bottom crust)

4 cups flour
1 cup + 3 tablespoons shortening
2/3–1/2 cup cold water
1 tablespoon vinegar
1 large egg

In a bowl, cut shortening into flour until texture is mealy.

In a separate bowl, beat together water, vinegar, and egg.

Combine flour and egg mixture using a fork. If the dough is not moist enough, add a little more water or if necessary add flour.

Divide into four pieces and roll out each piece, flouring both the rolling surface and the rolling pin. Place crusts into two greased pie dishes. Set aside.

Apple Filling:
6–10 apples
1/2 cup white sugar
1 teaspoon cinnamon
1/2 teaspoon nutmeg
1 tablespoon butter

Peel and core apples. Quarter the apples and make apple slices from each quarter. Add sugar and spices to apples. Pour apple mixture into prepared bottom crust. Dot with 1 tablespoon of butter. Cover with top crust. Make slits in crust. Mask the edges of the pie with foil.

Bake at 425 degrees for 45–60 minutes or until juicy and lightly browned. (You may also microwave the pie for 11 minutes and then bake it at 425 degrees for about 20 minutes).

## ANISE BISCOTTI
MAKES 2 DOZEN

3 eggs
1/2 cup shortening
1 cup sugar
1 teaspoon pure anise extract
4 cups flour
6 teaspoons baking powder
3/4 cup milk
1 egg for wash

In a bowl, combine eggs, shortening, sugar, and anise.

In a separate bowl, combine flour, baking powder, and milk.

Combine flour mixture with egg mixture. Work with hands until dough is smooth.

Shape the dough into 4 logs and place on a cookie sheet. Brush with a beaten egg. Place the logs on a cookie sheet covered with parchment paper.

Bake at 400 degrees until slightly brown. Slice and turn the slices on their sides. Return to the oven to toast for about 3 minutes.

For Lemon Biscotti, use 5 tablespoons of lemon flavor instead of anise extract. Frost with sugar icing (see page 100).

*L*orraine Louanis is the daughter of one of the last schooner captains, Francis Joseph Hynes, a Newfoundlander, from Fortune Bay. He arrived in "The Boston States" in the mid-1920s, already a seasoned seaman. In the years that followed, Hynes fished on or skippered some of Gloucester and Boston's most famous dory trawlers, including the *Gertrude de Costa, Gertrude L. Thebaud, Mary E. O'Hara, Shamrock, Marjorie Parker,* and *Grand Marshall.* In 1952, he took a site on a Boston beam trawler. The following year, his cousin, Leo Hynes, retired the *Adventure*, ending the celebrated age of schooners.

As a girl, Lorraine frequently accompanied her father to the Boston Fish Pier to help him and other schooner captains to fill out their boat logs. She assisted crewmen to read important documents and letters, too. Her father read but barely wrote. He was self-educated as was her mother, the former Mary Lucille Powers, also a native Newfoundlander, who worked as a domestic for Dr. Frank Lahey, founder of the Lahey Clinic.

In Boston in the late 1930s and early 1940s, Lorraine remembers seeing "not only schooners, but seiners and beam trawlers. The boats were tied up two and three abreast. We had to walk over one to get to another." Her glimpses of life aboard the boats surprised and fascinated her: "The men cleaned themselves and everything else by using one of the few facilities available—the bucket. There was a bucket for everything—for toiletries, dishes, and garbage. Everything went over the side of the boat."

"The men stood around a pot bellied stove smoking their pipes and chewing tobacco. They would spit in a spittoon sitting beside the stove. In summertime, when the dogfish would strike, the men would develop boils on their hands and arms under their oilskins; they'd have sores from handling the dogfish while pulling their lines into the dories."

"The crew used to wear these heavy wool mittens and socks made by the women in Newfoundland; the women sheared the sheep and they carded and spun the wool. They used to make the mittens oversize and they would boil them to shrink them and then dip them in oil to make them impenetrable to weather."

Lorraine celebrated her 10th birthday aboard ship in Gloucester Harbor. At the time, her father was skippering the schooner *Shamrock* for the Boston-based O'Hara fleet. That day the 147-foot vessel was tied up at the dock where the Gloucester House stands today. "The engineer and cook made me a birthday cake with all this whipped cream. But they must have forgotten to wash their hands. It tasted like diesel oil! I ate it because I didn't want to hurt their feelings."

When Lorraine's father needed to talk privately to a boat owner, he sometimes dropped her off at the movies in Boston's Scolly Square, now Government Center. "He'd bring me to a seat up on the right hand side of the theatre and sit me down and tell me to wait till he got back. Admission was 10 cents and some people stayed there all night because they had nowhere else to stay."

As a fisherman's daughter, Lorraine was keenly aware of the sea's perils. So was her mother: "I remember nights when there would be bad storms. Mother would wake us up and we would recite the rosary before the statue of the Blessed Mother and a small statue of St. Theresa. When Dad lost a man, my mother would visit the widow. When a man would drown the hat was passed at the pier for the widow and children."

"There is an Irish saying," Lorraine says, "What the sea wants it gets." More than once, her father narrowly escaped disaster. "He should have been on the *Commonwealth* when, in 1927, the schooner's gasoline engine exploded killing all but five men." At the time, Francis Joseph Hynes was in the hospital having surgery for an old WW I injury. Then in 1941, not long after he had turned over command of the *Mary E. O'Hara*, she struck an unlit coal barge, and sank, laden with fish, while steaming into port. Of her 23-man crew, only five survived.

Lorraine married outside the fishing industry. She and her husband, Edgar Roger Louanis, had two children.

## SALMON ROLL WITH EGG SAUCE
SERVES 3–4

Dough:
2 cups flour
4 tablespoons baking powder
1/2 teaspoon salt
1 egg, slightly beaten
1/2 cup milk
4 tablespoons shortening

Filling:
1 lb. fresh salmon, cut into small pieces
4 tablespoons milk
2 tablespoons lemon juice
1 1/2 tablespoons parsley, chopped
1/2 teaspoon salt

White Sauce:
2 cups warm milk
2 tablespoons flour
4 tablespoons butter
1 teaspoon salt
1/4 teaspoon pepper
2 hard-boiled eggs, chopped
2 teaspoons parsley

*The schooner* Alabama *in Gloucester Harbor*
Photo courtesy of Sharon's Studio of Gloucester

In a bowl, sift together flour, baking powder, salt, and shortening. Mix well with a fork.

In a separate bowl, combine egg, milk, and shortening. Combine with flour mixture. Mix well and roll out onto a floured board 8 inches long, 1/4" thick. Roll the dough as you would for a jelly roll.

In a separate bowl, combine salmon, milk, lemon juice, parsley, and salt. Mix well and spread evenly on the dough.

Place on a greased baking sheet and bake at 400 degrees for 30 minutes.

Melt butter in a medium saucepan. Add flour, salt, and pepper. Stir to a paste. Add milk and bring to a boil for 3 minutes. Remove from heat and add eggs and parsley. Serve over salmon.

"I did not want to marry an Italian or a fisherman. I ended up doing both," says Mary Brancaleone, "and I'm very happy that I did."

As a young girl growing up in Gloucester in the 1950s, Mary enjoyed the warm embrace of a large Sicilian-American family. She had good friends in her Addison Street neighborhood, an enclave of Italian descendants. But in school, Mary "felt different because my mother did not speak English. I used to get mad at her because she couldn't speak with my teachers. I especially wanted her to meet my third grade teacher. Mrs. Taylor was a great teacher and lived up the street from us. One Sunday my mother made spaghetti and meat sauce and we brought it to Mrs. Taylor. That was one of the highlights of my childhood!"

A good student and talented athlete, Mary served as captain of the eighth-grade girls basketball team. In high school, however, where cliques abounded, she struggled against prejudice. "Italians were looked down upon as lower class." Mary did not make any team, passed over in favor of "the American kids."

Mary wanted simply to fit in. As a schoolgirl, she had little interest in speaking Sicilian or in hearing stories about life in Terrasini, Sicily, during World War II. Her mother, Catherine Ciolino, and older brothers, Sam, Tony, and Joe, spent the war years in Terrasini waiting to emigrate, while her father, Dominic Ciolino, fished off Gloucester. In spring, 1946, the family reunited in Gloucester. Mary was born that December, a generation after her brothers.

In Gloucester, Mary's mother quickly became known for her culinary skills, especially her baking. "She was an amazing baker. She made *pignolata*,

*sfinge, biscotti, cucciddata*, and her own special lemon cookies. She loved baking and she had a special knack. She could feel the texture of the dough and know if it needed more sugar or Crisco. And she had a certain style. When people saw her cookies, they knew they were hers," says Mary. "The church sold them at their fair, and she brought them to the police, the pharmacist, and all her neighbors."

On St. Joseph's feast day, Catherine Ciolino served the famous pasta, with her own special linguine, to 60 to 70 people, family and friends, who crowded into her house. The feast culminated a nine-day novena, which Catherine began offering during the Korean War in order to pray for all those in the Service. Mary's mother also loved to garden and to do needlepoint. "She was a true homemaker."

Always independent, Mary set her sights elsewhere. After graduating from Gloucester High School, she became a hairdresser and attended college at night to receive an associate's degree in business administration. Having grown up in a fishing family, she insisted that she "did not want that kind of life," in which the men are at sea long days and weeks at a time. Then one New Year's Eve, she wound up on a double date with Tom (Gaetano) Brancaleone. They fell in love, married, had three children, and he continued fishing until retiring eight years ago.

"When we were first married, my husband would be out fishing for eight to ten days and we never heard a word. We would go through storms and we did not know if he was alive," says Mary. "From a fisherman's wife's perspective, the biggest change in the industry involves" ship-to-shore communication. Prior to cell (and satellite) phones, fishermen relied largely on marine radio, and often a boat's owner was the only one with a land-based receiver. When Tom Brancaleone bought his own boat, the *Paul and Dominic*, he immediately installed a VHF receiver at home. The marine radio not only facilitated communication between the Brancaleones, it brought the sea's perils ever more vividly into Mary's daily life. When it was stormy or a boat was in trouble, one fisherman's wife called another and told her to monitor Channel 16, the emergency channel. The women stood around the crackling receiver drinking coffee, listening, and waiting for word that their husbands were safe. "How we all worried; if something happened we all got together."

"I was very happy when Tom retired," says Mary. When he was fishing, she did the books for that business, while maintaining the household, raising their three children, and working part time as a hairdresser. Today she works as a real estate agent while serving as the clerk and an active member of the Gloucester Fishermen's Wives Association. She fundraised for the Fishermen's Wives Memorial, and, over the years, she has helped coordinate the GFWA's many cooking demonstrations, aimed at promoting the consumption of underutilized species at seafood festivals, street fairs, and supermarkets including Bread & Circus, Stop & Shop, and Trader Joe's. "We'd prepare the herring patties or the pollock in Gloucester and then bake or fry the fish at the stores so people could see it cooking and taste it."

Today Mary organizes a crew of fishermen's wives, from the GFWA and the Sicilian Society, to provide two meals a year at the Open Door, Gloucester's food pantry. The women procure donations of fresh fish. Last fall, they cooked and served 75 people, making this one of the Open Door's most popular meals.

Two years ago, on a GFWA exchange program in Tamano, Japan, Mary found herself conducting a cooking class for 50 Japanese men and women at that City's Civic Center. With help from Angela Sanfilippo's daughter, Giovanna, Mary assisted her students to prepare *calamari* with spaghetti. "We spoke English and we had a translator. It was hilarious trying to translate.

Sometimes the words don't come out the same. But the people absolutely loved it, and they were so appreciative and friendly; they were just wonderful."

Some of Mary's fondest memories are of St. Peter's fiesta. "When I was a kid it was a great thing. You got new clothes for those four days. You got to go on the rides and a couple of times we were in the procession." Neither of her sons became fishermen, but Paul, 36, of Gloucester, still walks the greasy pole and till recently his brother, Dominic, 33, had joined him; for Dominic this now requires traveling cross-country from California where he lives with his young family. Rosandra, 26, the Brancaleone's youngest, also returns for this celebration of the fishermen's saint.

Today, as her own children, all college graduates, are forging lives of their own, Mary looks nostalgically at the close-knit immigrant life that she knew as a child. She sees the bitter sweetness of the passing of an era: "Kids today don't have the close ties to family that we did." Increasingly, she treasures her own religious and cultural traditions as a Sicilian-American. While she once sought, above all, to fit in as an American, today she's become a strong defender of her own priceless heritage.

*The Blessing of the Fleet*

## PASTICCIOTTI
**Italian cookie filled with ricotta**
MAKES 4–5 DOZEN

8 cups flour
2 tablespoons baking powder
2 1/2 cups sugar
3 cups shortening
4 eggs
1 cup milk
1 teaspoon vanilla

Filling:
See page 45 for cream filling
1 lb. ricotta
1/2 cup sugar
1 lemon rind, grated
1 teaspoon cinnamon
chocolate chips to taste (optional)
confectioners' sugar

In a bowl, combine flour, baking powder, sugar, and shortening with your hands until shortening is dissolved.

In a blender, beat eggs and vanilla. Add to flour mixture and then gradually add milk. Mixture should be soft and smooth.

Roll out dough until it is about 1/2" thick. Cut out circles using a wide glass. Add about 1 tablespoon of filling to each circle. Fold in half and press edges together. Place cookies on a greased cookie sheet and bake at 300 degrees for about 10 minutes or until cookies are lightly browned. Sprinkle with confectioners' sugar.

*The fishing vessel* Merganser *covered in ice in Gloucester Harbor*
Photo courtesy of Donald R. Mason

For filling, make the cream filling on page 45. Refrigerate until cool. Place pudding in a food processor for about 2 minutes. Add ricotta and blend for another 2–3 minutes or until smooth. Remove pudding and place in a bowl. Add sugar, lemon peel, cinnamon, and chocolate chips. Adjust taste as needed.

## SPIEDINI
MAKES 2–3 DOZEN

3 lb. eye round roast, sliced very thin (ask grocer to slice)
seasoned Italian bread crumbs
extra virgin olive oil
1 28-oz. can crushed tomatoes
1/4 can water
1 lb. hard Romano cheese
salt and pepper
4 large onions, sliced
rounded toothpicks

Heat oil in a skillet and sauté onions. Add crushed tomatoes, water, and salt and pepper to taste. Simmer for about 20 minutes. Remove from heat.

While sauce is cooking, pound meat and clean off fatty edges. Bread meat by dipping in oil and then bread crumbs. Set aside.

Cut cheese into small carrot-like slices.

Lay breaded meat flat. Place one teaspoon of sauce and one piece of cheese down the center of each piece of meat. Fold in sides around roll. Fasten with a toothpick. Broil on both sides for about 5 minutes or until golden brown.

"Easter was a very special day in my parents' house, especially for us children," says 83-year Margaret Ferraro Favazza. "That morning we waited eagerly for my mother to cut the *pizza ghina*, the stuffed pizza that she had made on Good Friday. Tradition has it that you cannot cut the pizza till Easter morning, which can be a long wait for a child. My sisters and cousins and I still keep the tradition today."

"To make the *pizza ghina*, we make our own dough just like my mother did. We fill it with prosciutto, eggs, and a special ricotta (which you can buy in Gloucester only at Easter.)"

The stuffed pizza is a specialty of Naples, the home of Margaret's parents and, possibly, of pizza itself. Pizza has been the food of Naples since the 18th century. To Neapolitans it is "a grace note of life, a subtle piece of magic transmuted by the alchemy of fire into a delicacy for the nose, the mouth, and the eyes," observes Carol Field in her now classic book, *The Italian Baker*.

Another Easter favorite is Margaret's sweet bread. "I've been making it for years, ever since my children were young. They all loved it toasted. I work everything by hand. It's very light and delicious!"

Margaret makes one large round braided loaf, which she decorates with colored hard boiled Easter eggs and places on the table as a centerpiece. She makes smaller loaves for her children and grandchildren. Orange extract, orange juice, and orange peel flavor the light yeast bread. The sweet bread reflects the combined Portuguese and Italian cultural influences of the East Cambridge neighborhood where Margaret grew up and of Gloucester, where she lives today. A version of her sweet bread recipe originally

came from her sister. When they were growing up, their mother made a Neapolitan sweet bread at Easter using a cookie dough.

A gracious woman with a lovely smile, Margaret is always in the kitchen baking, cooking, preparing old family recipes. "I love to cook. I make everything," says Margaret. The week before Thanksgiving, she made her own ravioli, which she froze for the holiday. Several days later she was planning to make *gnocchi*. Besides the traditional potato *gnocchi* of Northern Italy, Margaret prepares a *gnocchi* with ricotta and a fine-ground semolina flour.

But pizza is her favorite. "I've always made pizza. I can whip it up in no time. I learned to make it from my mother." Margaret used to help out making pizza at Sebastian's in Gloucester and for seven years she put in long hours at a pizza shop that her son ran in nearby Beverly.

Margaret's parents, Luigi and Rosaria Ferraro, were born and raised in Tarauni, a mountain village north of Naples. "When my mother was growing up, the only way to travel there was by donkey cart. My grandparents farmed. They had chestnut and hazelnut trees and they would go to the market and sell the nuts. They weren't rich, but they were comfortable and healthy. They didn't have running water in the house. The water came out of a spigot in the mountain. It was clear spring water."

Margaret was born and grew up in East Cambridge during the Depression. "My father was a laborer. He made $18 a week. We were fortunate because we had an income. Many others were forced to go to soup kitchens. We also had property. That's the one thing about the immigrants. They worked and they got property. They all bought big houses.

*The fishing vessel* Jean D'Arc

My father bought a six-family house and sold that and bought another six-family. One uncle opened a grocery store; he cut his own meat. Two other uncles, who worked in foundries, decided they wanted to go into farming. They bought farms out in Randolph [MA]. They made a living out of that, just the few months in the summer and raised families on that."

"When I was growing up, one of my jobs was to go down cellar and stack the wood. My father chopped it and me and my four sisters stacked it in the summer. Then in winter we carried baskets of wood and buckets of coal up to the third floor. We lived in five rooms on the third floor—me and my parents, sisters, and our little brother. My mother banked the stove at night. The stove burned wood and coal and was our only source of heat. We girls always helped our mother. She had so much to do— cooking and cleaning and taking care of all of us. Our

*Our Lady of Good Voyage Church*
Photo courtesy of Sharon's Studio of Gloucester

father, God bless him, did all the shopping. He was a great shopper!"

"I went to Catholic grammar school through eighth grade. My parents wanted me to finish, but I quit high school because I wanted to make money. I went into stitching." From ages 16 to 21, Margaret worked at Paul Drago & Company in Boston making draperies, curtains, and bed spreads. Later she machine embroidered ladies' dresses at the Washington Art Company in Boston.

At age 21 she married Serafino Favazza, a Sicilian-American fisherman from Boston's North End. Soon after they moved to Gloucester. "We landed in Gloucester because my husband was a commercial fisherman. Gloucester was a better place to fish from. I would never go back to the City."

Serafino captained such boats as the *Julie Ann, Raymonde,* and *Jean D'Arc,* while also earning his captain's license and teaching navigation for many years. Margaret managed the accounts for the house and boat and raised their two daughters and son. In the late 1940s, she learned to drive. My sister-in-law drove first, a little bit before me. That was the time we were coming out of our shells." Margaret and Serafino enjoyed 42 years of marriage, until his death at age 65.

Margaret has been a mainstay of the Gloucester Fishermen's Wives Association.

"She has always been there for the Wives and the fishing community," says Angela Sanfilippo, the GFWA's president. "And Margaret is a very giving person. When my daughter Mary Ann was getting married we needed a basket for the gift envelopes. Margaret asked, 'what color are the girls' dresses?' 'She brought us a beautiful basket she made with lilac flowers and satin ribbons. We used it for both the shower and wedding."

## CHOCOLATE CHIP BISCOTTI

MAKES 2 DOZEN

2 cups flour
1 teaspoon baking powder
1 teaspoon ground cinnamon
1/8 teaspoon salt
1/2 cup butter at room temperature
1/2 cup firmly packed brown sugar
1/2 cup granulated sugar
1 tablespoon instant espresso powder
2 eggs
1 cup walnuts, chopped
1 cup chocolate chips

In a bowl, combine flour, baking powder, cinnamon, and salt. Set aside.

In a separate bowl, use an electric mixer to cream butter, brown sugar, white sugar, and espresso powder. Add eggs one at a time. Add flour mixture and continue mixing for 2 minutes. Mix in walnuts and chocolate chips with a spoon.

Divide dough into 3 portions. Form 3 logs and place on a cookie sheet covered with parchment paper. Bake at 325 degrees for 25 minutes. Remove from sheet and cut diagonally into 1/2" slices. Place back in the oven and brown on each side for 10 minutes.

## TIRAMISU TOFFEE TRIFLE PIE

MAKES 8-10 SERVINGS

1 1/2 tablespoons instant coffee granules
3/4 cup warm water
1 10-oz. frozen pound cake, thawed
1 8-oz. package cream cheese or mascarpone, softened
1/2 cup powdered sugar
1/2 cup chocolate syrup
1 12-oz. container frozen whipped topping, thawed and divided
2 1.4-oz. English toffee candy bars, coarsely chopped

Stir together coffee granules and 3/4 cup warm water until granules are dissolved. Cool.

Cut pound cake into 14 slices. Cut each slice in half diagonally. Place triangles on the bottom and against the sides of a 9" deep-dish pie plate. Drizzle coffee over cake.

Beat cream cheese, sugar, and chocolate syrup at medium speed with an electric mixer until smooth. Add 2 1/2 cups whipped topping and beat until light and fluffy.

Spread cheese mixture evenly over cake. Dollop remaining whipped topping around edges of pie. Sprinkle with chopped candy. Chill 8 hours.

**Note:** Tiramisu Toffee Trifle Pie may be made the day before serving. Store in refrigerator.

## AUNT GEN'S BISCOTTI

MAKES 4 DOZEN

6 eggs
1 1/2 cups sugar
1/2 cup oil
3 tablespoons vanilla
4 cups flour
3 tablespoons baking powder
1 lb. candied fruit (optional)

In a bowl, beat together eggs, sugar, vanilla, and oil. Add flour, baking powder, and fruit. Knead together to make the dough. Divide into four portions and form logs. Place on a greased cookie sheet. Brush tops with egg yolks.

Bake at 350 degrees for 20 minutes. Cut logs into 1" slices with a large bread knife.

## MARGARET'S EASTER SWEET BREAD

5 lbs. flour
1 dozen eggs, beaten
4 oranges, juice and grated peels
1 lb. butter, melted
2 cups warm milk
4 yeast cakes
3 cups sugar
1 small bottle orange or rum extract

Place flour in a large bowl and make a well. In a separate bowl, beat eggs, butter, and orange juice, extract, and peels. Mix together milk, yeast, sugar, and extract. Pour egg and milk mixtures into the well and knead for about 20 minutes.

Cover dough with a towel and let rise for 2 hours. Divide dough into 6 portions and place in 9" pie pans. Let them rise in the pan for about 20 minutes covered with a towel.

Brush with egg yolks and bake at 400 degrees for 30 minutes or until golden brown.

## LARGE WHITE CAKE

5 egg whites
2 cups sugar, divided
2 1/2 cups flour
2/3 cup shortening
1 cup milk
1 1/2 teaspoons vanilla or almond extract

In a bowl, beat egg whites until stiff with 1/2 cup sugar.

In a separate bowl, use an electric mixer to cream together 1 1/2 cups sugar, shortening, milk, and vanilla. Add flour and mix. Gently fold in the egg whites.

Pour batter into 2 greased 9" cake pans. Bake at 350 degrees for 40 minutes.

## DATE NUT CAKE

1 cup sugar
1 cup shortening
1 egg
1 cup water
1 teaspoon vanilla extract
1/4 teaspoon salt
1 2/3 cups flour
1 teaspoon baking soda
1 cup walnuts
1 cup dates

In a bowl, cream together sugar, shortening, egg, water, and vanilla.

In a separate bowl, combine flour, salt, baking soda, nuts, and dates. Combine with creamed mixture. Blend well and pour into a greased 9" x 13" pan. Bake at 350 degrees for 1 hour.

Dust with confectioners' sugar.

## CREAM CHEESE BROWNIES
MAKES 1-1/2 DOZEN

4 oz. unsweetened chocolate squares
4 oz. semisweet chocolate squares
1/3 cup butter or margarine
1-8 oz. package cream cheese, softened
1/4 cup butter or margarine, softened
2 cups sugar, divided
6 large eggs, divided
3 teaspoons vanilla extract, divided
1 1/2 cups (9oz.) semisweet chocolate morsels, divided
1 cup + 2 tablespoons all purpose flour, divided
1 teaspoon baking powder
1 teaspoon salt

Microwave the first 3 ingredients in a 1-quart glass bowl on high for 2 minutes or until melted, stirring once. Cool mixture.

Beat cream cheese and butter at medium speed with an electric mixer until creamy. Gradually add 1/2 cup sugar, beating until blended. Stir in 1 teaspoon vanilla. Fold in 2 tablespoons of flour and 1/2 cup chocolate morsels; set aside.

Beat remaining 4 eggs in a large bowl at medium speed with an electric mixer. Gradually add remaining 1-1/2 cups sugar, beating well. Add melted chocolate mixture and remaining 2 teaspoons vanilla extract. Beat mixture until well blended.

Combine 1 cup flour, baking powder, and salt. Fold into chocolate batter until blended and stir in remaining cup of chocolate morsels.

Reserve 2 cups chocolate batter. Spread remaining batter evenly in a greased 13" x 9" pan. Pour cream cheese mixture over batter in pan. Top with reserved 2 cups chocolate batter.

## POUND CAKE

6 large eggs
2 cups sugar
1 1/2 cups shortening
3 cups flour
1/2 cup milk
1/2 teaspoon salt
2 teaspoons vanilla
1 teaspoon baking powder

Using an electric mixer, cream together eggs, sugar, and shortening. Add flour, milk, salt, vanilla, and baking powder. Beat for 20 minutes.

Pour batter into a greased and floured 12" x 5" loaf pan. Bake at 350 degrees for 1 hour.

Cool for 10 minutes before removing from pan.

## BLUEBERRY MUFFINS
MAKES 20 MUFFINS

2 cups flour
1/4 cup sugar
1 tablespoon baking powder
1/2 teaspoon salt
1 cup milk
1/4 cup vegetable oil
1 large egg, lightly beaten
1 cup fresh or frozen blueberries

Combine flour and next 3 ingredients in a large mixing bowl. Make a well in center of mixture. In a separate bowl, cream together milk, vegetable oil, and egg. Add to dry ingredients and mix until moistened. Gently fold in blueberries.

Spoon batter evenly into lightly greased muffin pans, filling 2/3 full. Bake at 400 degrees for 20–25 minutes.

## PIZZA CHIINA
### (Stuffed Easter Pizza)
SERVES 6

Filling:
3-lb. container ricotta cheese
1 cup grated Parmesean cheese
7 eggs, beaten
1 lb. prosciutto, small cubes
1/4 teaspoon pepper
2-lb. container fresh farm ricotta cheese, sliced

Mix first 5 ingredients together until well blended. Set aside.

Crust:
5 cups flour
1 teaspoon salt
1 tablespoon coarse black pepper
3 yeast cakes
1 cup warm water (add more if needed)
1/4 cup cooking oil
1 egg for wash

Combine all ingredients for crust and knead for 15 minutes.

Shape dough into a ball and cover with a towel, leaving it in a warm place. Let stand for 1 hour while dough rises.

Cut dough in half. Roll out bottom and top crusts very thin, like a pie crust.

Grease a 9" x 13" pan lightly with shortening. Place crust in bottom of pan, overlapping all sides. Add cheese filling. Top with sliced ricotta cheese. Cover with the top crust and seal all sides.

Egg wash:
Beat 1 egg. Brush egg wash on top of crust. Cut 5 air packets in crust. Bake at 325 degrees for 1 hour or until golden brown.

## ITALIAN MACARONI AND CHEESE
MAKES 8–10 SERVINGS

This rich, creamy dish calls for just about 20 minutes of hands–on work.

1 8-oz. package large elbow macaroni
1/2 cup Italian seasoned bread crumbs, divided
1 10-oz. block white cheddar cheese, shredded
2 cups mozzarella cheese, shredded
1/2 cup Parmesan cheese, shredded
6 large eggs, lightly beaten
4 cups milk
1 teaspoon salt
1 teaspoon pepper

Prepare macaroni according to package directions. Set aside.

Coat bottom and sides of a 13" x 9" baking dish with cooking spray. Sprinkle 1/4 cup bread crumbs evenly over bottom of baking dish, tilting dish to coat sides evenly with bread crumbs.

Layer one-third elbow macaroni, one-third shredded cheeses, and one-third remaining bread crumbs in baking dish. Repeat layers twice, ending with bread crumbs.

Whisk together eggs and next 3 ingredients. Pour evenly over layered mixture.

Bake at 350 degrees for 55 to 60 minutes or until golden and set. Let stand 10 minutes before serving. Sprinkle evenly with Tomato Basil Topping.

Tomato Basil Topping:
MAKES ABOUT 2 CUPS

4 large plum tomatoes, seeded and diced
1/4 cup Parmesan cheese, shredded
3 tablespoons fresh basil, chopped

Stir together all ingredients.

## SPICY VEGETABLES WITH PENNE PASTA

SERVES 6

You can tone down the heat by choosing a less spicy pasta sauce.

1/2 cup sun dried tomatoes
1/2 cup boiling water
12 oz. penne pasta
2 medium onions, chopped
2 small zucchinis, chopped
1 green bell pepper, chopped
1 red bell pepper, chopped
1 cup fresh mushrooms, sliced
2 garlic cloves, minced
2 tablespoons olive oil
1 26-oz. jar hot and spicy pasta sauce
1/2 cup chopped fresh basil
1/2 teaspoon salt

Stir together dried tomatoes and 1/2 cup boiling water in a bowl. Let stand 30 minutes. Drain, chop, and set aside.

Heat oil in a skillet and sauté next five ingredients until vegetables are tender. Stir in dried tomatoes.

Stir in pasta sauce, and bring to a boil. Reduce heat to medium. Add the basil and cook for about 15 minutes.

In the meantime, prepare pasta according to directions. Drain and top with sauce.

## MONKEY BREAD BITES

MAKES 1 DOZEN

1/2 cup granulated sugar, divided
1 tablespoon ground cinnamon
1 12-oz. can refrigerated Pillsbury buttermilk biscuits
1 6-oz. can refrigerated Pillsbury buttermilk biscuits
1/2 cup + 2 tablespoons butter
1/2 cup firmly packed light brown sugar
1 teaspoon vanilla extract
1/2 cup chopped pecans, toasted
extra-large foil muffin cups

Combine 1/4 cup granulated sugar and cinnamon in a large bowl. Cut biscuits into fourths, and add to sugar mixture. Toss to coat. Set aside.

Melt butter in medium saucepan over medium heat. Add brown sugar and remaining 1/4 cup granulated sugar, stirring until sugar dissolves. Remove from heat. Stir in vanilla and pecans.

Arrange 5 coated biscuit pieces in a lightly greased foil muffin cup. Place in a muffin pan. Repeat with remaining biscuit pieces. Drizzle evenly with pecan mixture.

Bake at 400 degrees for 18 minutes or until golden.

ETHEL PADRE
## PORTUGUESE SWEET BREAD

3 cups milk
1 stick butter
3 packages yeast
1/3 cup water, lukewarm
3 cups sugar
1 dozen extra-large eggs
5 lbs. flour

In a saucepan, melt butter in milk over low heat until warm.

Add yeast to lukewarm water until dissolved.

In a separate bowl, cream together sugar and eggs until smooth.

In a separate bowl, combine the flour with the milk and butter mixture. Add yeast to the egg and sugar mixture. Knead dough until smooth. This takes a little time and muscle. Cover with a warm towel, then layer on a cloth tablecloth, and finally a blanket.

Let rise 3–4 hours.

Grease loaf pans with shortening. Do not use flour.

Divide dough into 6 portions and place in 9" pie plates. Bake at 350 degrees for 30 minutes or until done.

*Gloucester City Hall*
Photo by Alan Murtagh

## CODFISH CAKES
SERVES 4

1 box salted codfish
3 tablespoons onion, chopped
1/2 teaspoon nutmeg
1/2 teaspoon allspice
1/2 teaspoon pepper
1/2 teaspoon cinnamon
3 potatoes

Soak codfish in water overnight. Change water and then bring to a boil. Once boiling, remove fish and taste to see if it is still too salty. If too salty, place in fresh water and bring to boil again. Do this until salt has been reduced in the fish. It may take 3 boils.

In a separate saucepan, boil potatoes until tender. Mash the potatoes and then combine all ingredients. Shape into round patties, and fry until golden brown. Let drain on paper towel.

Serve and enjoy!

## VIN A DAISE MARINADE (Ving a Thize)

1 teaspoon salt
1/2 teaspoon crushed red pepper
2 garlic cloves, chopped
2 cups cider vinegar
1 cup water

Combine ingredients for marinade. Pour over pork chops and marinate for 8–12 hours. Bake, fry, or broil. Delicious!!

## GRANNY'S CHICKEN SOUP
SERVES 4–6

2 chicken breasts on bone
2 cumin seeds
1 teaspoon salt
1/2 teaspoon allspice
1 tablespoon parsley
1 onion, chopped
1/2 teaspoon cinnamon
4 potatoes, cubed

Place chicken in soup pan along with spices and cover with water. Bring to a boil and cook until chicken is tender. Remove from pan and take chicken off of bone. Add the cubed potatoes into the chicken broth and continue boiling until potatoes are almost done. Add chicken to the pan and continue cooking until potatoes are soft. Delicious!!

ROSOLIE RUZZO
## ANTIPASTO
SERVES 4–6

1 large box whole mushrooms
1/2 teaspoon garlic, crushed
1 celery stalk, cut into medium-size pieces
2 cups of your favorite whole olives, pitted
1/2 lb. salami, cut into strips
3/4 lb. provolone cheese, cubed
1 4-oz. can anchovies
artichoke hearts, drained and quartered
1 tablespoon capers, rinsed
pepper, oregano, oil, and a little vinegar to taste

Place whole mushrooms in a saucepan with garlic and cover with water. Bring to a boil and then remove from heat immediately. Refrigerate. When you are ready to use them, drain and pat dry.

Place all ingredients in a bowl. Mix well and season

to taste.

FRANCES BUONOPANE
## MACARONI SALAD RICOTTA
SERVES 4–6

1/2 lb. whole wheat macaroni
1 cup ricotta cheese or cottage cheese
2 teaspoons wet mustard, thinned with yogurt*
mayonnaise
1/2 cup ripe olives, chopped
1 bell pepper, coarsely chopped
2 scallions, chopped
1 tablespoon parsley, chopped
red pimentos, to taste
1/2 teaspoon dill
1/2 teaspoon basil
salt and pepper to taste

Cook macaroni according to package directions. Drain and chill.

In a separate bowl, combine ricotta cheese and mustard.

Combine macaroni with cheese mixture. Add enough mayonnaise to moisten.

Add remaining ingredients.

Toss and serve on a bed of lettuce.

*Use yogurt, buttermilk, or milk to thin the mustard.

## MACEDONIAN SALAD
SERVES 4–6

1 large eggplant cut into 1" cubes, or smaller
4 tablespoons olive oil
2 tablespoons red wine vinegar
1 medium garlic clove, minced
1/2 teaspoon salt
freshly ground black pepper
1/2 cup parsley, finely minced
1/2 teaspoon basil

1/2 teaspoon thyme
1/2 teaspoon oregano
1/2 tablespoon fresh lemon juice
2 small scallions, very finely minced
1/2 medium red bell pepper, minced
1/2 medium green bell pepper, minced
1 medium tomato, diced
olives (greek, oil-cured, or nicoise)
yogurt
crumbled feta cheese

Preheat oven to 375 degrees. Spread eggplant cubes onto a lightly oiled baking tray. Bake for about 15 minutes, or until tender.

In a bowl, combine the olive oil, vinegar, garlic, salt, pepper, herbs, and lemon juice. Add the eggplant and stir. Cover and let sit for at least 2 hours.

Arrange remaining vegetables around the edge of a platter. Place the eggplant mixture in the middle. Serve garnished with olives and yogurt or feta cheese.

## RAFFAELA TERZO
## VEGETABLES AND RISOTTO TART
SERVES 4

3 cups cooked risotto
1 eggplant, sliced lengthwise
1 yellow pepper, seeded and cut in half
4 small tomatoes, chopped
4 tablespoons olive oil, divided
2 garlic cloves, finely chopped
1/2 cup black olives, pitted and chopped
1 sheet puff pastry, defrosted
salt and pepper to taste

Sprinkle salt on eggplant and let it set for 1 hour. Rinse in cold water, pat dry, and set aside.

Place the yellow pepper skin-side up on a sheet pan. Broil until skin begins to blacken. Peel, seed, and cut into long strips. Set aside.

Place eggplant on a greased sheet pan. Brush with a little olive oil and broil, turning occasionally, until tender and golden. Set aside.

Heat remaining olive oil in a skillet and sauté garlic until golden.

Add tomatoes and cook for 5 minutes. Add black olives and cook for another 5 minutes. Salt and pepper to taste. Remove from heat.

Grease a 9" x 5" x 3" pan. Layer eggplant, peppers, tomatoes, and olives evenly. Spread the risotto on top. Place the puff pastry on top of the risotto, tucking the overlap down inside the dish.

Bake at 375 degrees for 25–30 minutes or until the pastry is golden.

Cool slightly. Invert tart onto a large serving dish.

## BOILED SALMON WITH WHITE SAUCE
SERVES 4–6

2 lbs. fresh salmon
2 teaspoons salt
1/2 cup white wine vinegar

Sauce:
2 cups warm milk
4 tablespoons butter
2 tablespoons flour
1 teaspoon salt, to taste
1/4 teaspoon pepper

Place salmon in a small pot and cover with water. Add vinegar and salt. Bring to a boil and simmer for about 20 minutes.

Remove salmon from water. Remove skin. Place in a pie dish. Set aside.

Melt butter in a saucepan at medium heat. Add flour and salt and pepper. Stir together to form a paste.

Add warm milk. Bring to a boil, stirring constantly. Boil for 3 minutes. Pour over salmon and serve.

've brought along an old sea story that seems appropriate for this occasion, with a bit of poetic license: The good Lord was creating a model for Fishermen's wives and was into his 6th day of overtime when an angel appeared. She said, "Lord, you seem to be having some trouble with this one. What's wrong with the standard model?"

The Lord replied, "Have you seen the specifications for this order? The Fisherman's Wife has to be completely independent, possess the qualities of both father and mother, be a perfect hostess to four or forty with an hour's notice, handle every emergency imaginable without help, be able to carry on cheerfully, even if she is pregnant and has the flu, and she must be willing to endure months of separation from her husband. And, oh yes, she must have six pairs of hands."

The angel shook her head. "Six pairs of hands? No way." The Lord continued, "Don't worry, we will make other Fishermen's Wives to help her. And we will give her an unusually strong heart so it can swell with pride at her husband's achievements, sustain the pain of separations, beat soundly when it is overworked and tired, and be large enough to say, "I understand," when she doesn't, and say "I love you," regardless.

"Lord," said the angel, touching his arm gently, "Go to bed and get some rest, you can finish tomorrow." "I can't stop now," said the Lord. "I am so close to creating something unique. Already this model heals herself when she is sick, can put up six unexpected guests for the weekend, wave goodbye to her husband from a pier, and understand why it's important that he leave."

The angel circled the model of the Fisherman's Wife, looked at it closely and sighed, "It looks fine but it's too soft." "She might be soft," replied the Lord, "But she has the strength of a lion, you would not believe what she can endure."

Finally the angel bent over and ran her fingers across the cheek of the Lord's creation. "There's a leak" "Something is wrong with the construction. I'm not surprised that it has cracked. You are trying to put too much into this model." The Lord appeared offended at the angel's lack of confidence. "What you see is not a leak," he said, "it's a tear."

"A tear? What is it there for?" asked the angel. The Lord replied, "It's for joy, sadness, pain, disappointment, loneliness, and dedication to all the values that she and her husband hold dear."

"You are a genius!" exclaimed the angel. The Lord looked puzzled and replied "I didn't put it there."

---

*On August 5, 2001, the Gloucester Fishermen's Wives Association dedicated a monument to
honor the women who have been, and are, the soul of the fishing communities.
The memorial plaza was designed by Ann Gilardi Johnson, daughter of a Gloucester fisherman. The
eight-foot bronze sculpture, created by Morgan Faulds Pike, captures the all too familiar pose of
"waiting-with-strength" known to those whose family members have chosen to go to sea.
Envisioned by the wives, mothers, daughters, and sisters of Gloucester fishermen, the memorial honors
the faith, diligence, and fortitude of the wives of fishermen and mariners everywhere.*

Photo courtesy of Sharon's Studio of Gloucester

139

Yes, the fishermen's wives of Gloucester are great cooks. However, they are also much more than that.

In 1969, a group of women lead by Lena Novello, Grace Favazza, and Gerri Lovasco formed what was to become the Gloucester Fishermen's Wives Association (GFWA). Their mission was to represent, respond to, and alleviate the many problems affecting the fishing industry. They also hoped to promote a better understanding of fish among consumers. As Lena Novello said, "We wanted a voice, we wanted to be heard." And heard they were.

One of the Association's first goals was to stop foreign vessels from fishing within 200 miles of the US coast. When this goal was achieved, the successive legislation became an example for other nations to follow. The members continued to act as voices of the industry by attending meetings, lobbying Congress, and filing various lawsuits. They also came to understand that if the Gloucester and New England commercial fishing industries were to survive, the ocean needed to be protected. The importance of this realization applied not only to the industry, but to all of the people of the world.

The GFWA went on to successfully advocate for new laws to stop oil drilling on Georges Bank, halt the placing of a tire reef outside of Gloucester Harbor, terminate ocean dumping, and shut down fish farming in the open oceans. At the New England Fisheries Management Council, they pushed for fair and equal regulations for all fishermen. The Wives have also supported the establishment of the Stellwagen Bank Marine Sanctuary and backed legislation banning U.S. factory trawlers from being within 200 miles of the coast.

The extensive partnerships cultivated by the GFWA can be largely held responsible for the Association's success. For example, the Wives convened the *Vision 2020* community planning process, which resulted in a plan of action for the Port of Glouces-

ter. They also helped found the Massachusetts Fishermen's Partnership, and have undertaken joint projects with fishermen and scientists to bring their worlds together. On a global level, the GFWA has sponsored an international conference for fishermen and their wives, along with becoming the U.S. East Coast representative to the World Forum of Fish Harvesters and Fish Workers in India.

Education is a high priority for the Wives, who have established a *Mentor Program* to inspire new career choices for young people. In addition, the GFWA has submitted archival material for storage at Harvard's Schleslinger Library, and even published a cookbook in collaboration with the Cape Ann League of Women Voters, which has sold over 100,000 copies. The cookbook, which is called *The Taste of Gloucester,* has a focus on promoting all fish species.

The GFWA makes a point of working towards the improvement of the lives of fisherman. They have advocated for safety training in partnership with the U.S. Coast Guard, and worked with the Massachusetts Fishermen's Partnership to create the Fishermen's Partnership Health Plan. Finally, they initiated the request for funding from the U.S. Department of Labor to establish three fishermen's centers in Massachusetts for retraining and employment services for fishermen, their families, and industry workers.

The work of the GFWA is not over; in fact, much more needs to be done. In order to integrate the Association's ongoing projects beneath one roof, a resource center has been established with an ongoing staff. Present projects include providing assistance to the children and wives of fishermen lost at sea, environmental protection and education, and economic and business development. The resource center also intends to create new programs, such as assisting in gaining access to training and education programs for fishermen and their families, providing career development and job

Photo courtesy of Sharon's Studio of Gloucester

development services, acting as a broker for channeling and networking resources, and raising public awareness concerning the fisheries and the marine habitat. What is more, they plan to hold cooking classes, increase their membership base, and develop the financial resources needed to sustain the work of the organization.

The GFWA invites others to join them in the fight for justice. This extends not only to fishing communities, but to all communities, and to the earth that we call our home. As the opening message by Angela Sanfilippo, the Association's president, reads in the program booklet for the dedication of the Gloucester Fishermen's Wives Memorial, "The spirit embodied in this memorial now invites you and all women of the world to stand together with the members of the GFWA to make sure that justice prevails and that the entire human race enjoys peace, freedom, and the pursuit of happiness."

Please join the GFWA in its work.

—Jeanne Gallo

To contribute to the GFWA or to contact the organization for more information, please call 978-282-1401, go to our website http://www.gfwa.org, or write to:

GFWA
GFWA Resource Center
11–15 Parker Street
Gloucester, MA 01930

If you are making a contribution, please make checks payable to either: Gloucester Fishermen's Wives Association (not tax deductible), Gloucester Fishermen's Wives Development Program, Inc. (tax deductible), or Gloucester Fishermen's Wives Memorial, Inc. (for maintenance of memorial).

# INDEX

# ACKNOWLEDGMENTS

This book started out as an oral history project initiated by the Gloucester Fishermen's Wives Association. Stella Price, who serves on the faculty at Gordon College, was hired to interview fishermen's wives and, with help from her students, Claire Collins, Ashley Fowler and Nathan Rinaldi, she then transcribed and shaped the interviews into oral histories.

Susan Pollack, the author of this book, further interviewed the Wives on the themes of cooking and activism. Drawing upon these interviews, her 25 years experience writing about fishing communities, together with Stella's interviews and oral histories, Susan wrote the *Gloucester Fishermen's Wives Cookbook*.

Stella graciously gave us permission to consult her interviews and oral histories of the women who have kept the Gloucester fishing industry alive. We acknowledge Stella's contribution, dedication, and faith in something that will live forever.

*

The Gloucester Fishermen's Wives Association also wishes to thank the 18 fishermen's wives who opened their lives and hearts to us for this book:

Nina Benson, Mary Brancaleone, Rosandra Brancaleone, Connie Condon, Priscilla Decker-Evans, Grace Favazza, Margaret Favazza, Ann Gilardi Johnson, Nina Groppo, Gerri Lovasco, Lorraine Louanis, Lena Novello, Margherita Pellicia, Estrela Randazzo, Sefatia Romeo, Angela Sanfilippo, Josephine Taormina, and Rosalie Vitale.

Our deepest gratitude goes to Eric Schoonover, whose love and cooking sustained the author during the writing of this book, Barbara Beckwith of the National Writers Union, Stephanie Morgan, and other close friends of the author for their encouragement and support.

Many have given generously of their time. Our sincere thanks to Nina Groppo, Angela Sanfilippo, and Raffaela Terzo for their culinary labors, specifically for preparing dishes for the photo shoot and for gathering and translating recipes.

We are also profoundly grateful to Franco Groppo (f/v *Miss Trish II*) and John Sanfilippo (f/v *Giovanna*) for providing the fish for the dishes photographed and for other assistance and support in putting together this book.

We deeply appreciate the generosity of Bruce Nicholls for his legal counsel.

Our sincere thanks to Sharon Beliveau, Francesca Dibenedetto, Jeanne Gallo, and Marsie Silvestro for recipes and other assistance.

We are very grateful to Jeff Rotman Photography for generously donating portraits of the fishermen.

*

We honor the memory of Mary Ann Pascucci Perry, Peggy Sibley, and Lena Novello and thank all GFWA members, past and present, for their dedication and support to our cause during the past 35 years.

*"When the tide goes in and out and the lighthouse in the harbor flashes, think of us."*

—Angela Sanfilippo, President
Gloucester Fishermen's Wives Association